HIDDEN HISTORY *of the* LLANO ESTACADO

HIDDEN HISTORY *of the* LLANO ESTACADO

Edited by Paul H. Carlson and David J. Murrah

THE History PRESS

Published by The History Press
Charleston, SC
www.historypress.net

Copyright © 2017 by Paul H. Carlson and David J. Murrah
All rights reserved

First published 2017

Manufactured in the United States

ISBN 9781625858863

Library of Congress Control Number: 2017948489

Notice: The information in this book is true and complete to the best of our knowledge. It is offered without guarantee on the part of the authors or The History Press. The authors and The History Press disclaim all liability in connection with the use of this book.

All rights reserved. No part of this book may be reproduced or transmitted in any form whatsoever without prior written permission from the publisher except in the case of brief quotations embodied in critical articles and reviews.

This book is dedicated to our mentors, three superior West Texas historians who were not afraid to tackle local history: Rupert N. Richardson, William C. Holden and Ernest Wallace.

Contents

Preface

Like the many beautiful canyons hiding in the folds of the caprock escarpment bordering it, the Llano Estacado has an abundance of hidden tales in its colorful history. After all, it is one of the most unique regions in the entire world—a treeless wind-swept flat plain that stretches for more than two hundred miles.

Known historically as the Llano Estacado, or Staked Plains, the region encompasses thirty-two thousand square miles of eastern New Mexico and the South Plains of Texas. It is home to nearly 1.2 million people. And it has been home to humans for over twelve thousand years.

Long before Europeans discovered the Llano, the first Native Americans ascended the high plains to hunt large animals that thrived on its grassy prairies—mammoths, bison, antelope and deer—all while being on foot. Eventually, Spanish explorers led by Francisco de Coronado in 1540–41 intruded, leaving behind Spanish-named places (place names), especially for water sources—the Brazos and Colorado Rivers, for example, and springs at *Casas Amarillas* and *Canon de Rescate* (Ransom Canyon).

But they also left horses, which rapidly multiplied and, in time, provided mounts for the indigenous bands of the Great Plains, especially Apaches and Comanches. By the mid-1700s, Comanches had become expert horsemen and warriors, and they drove all others from the flat and featureless landscape and rich hunting grounds of the Llano Estacado.

As a result, as American settlers pushed the frontier westward in the 1800s, particularly after the Mexican cession of vast lands in the Southwest

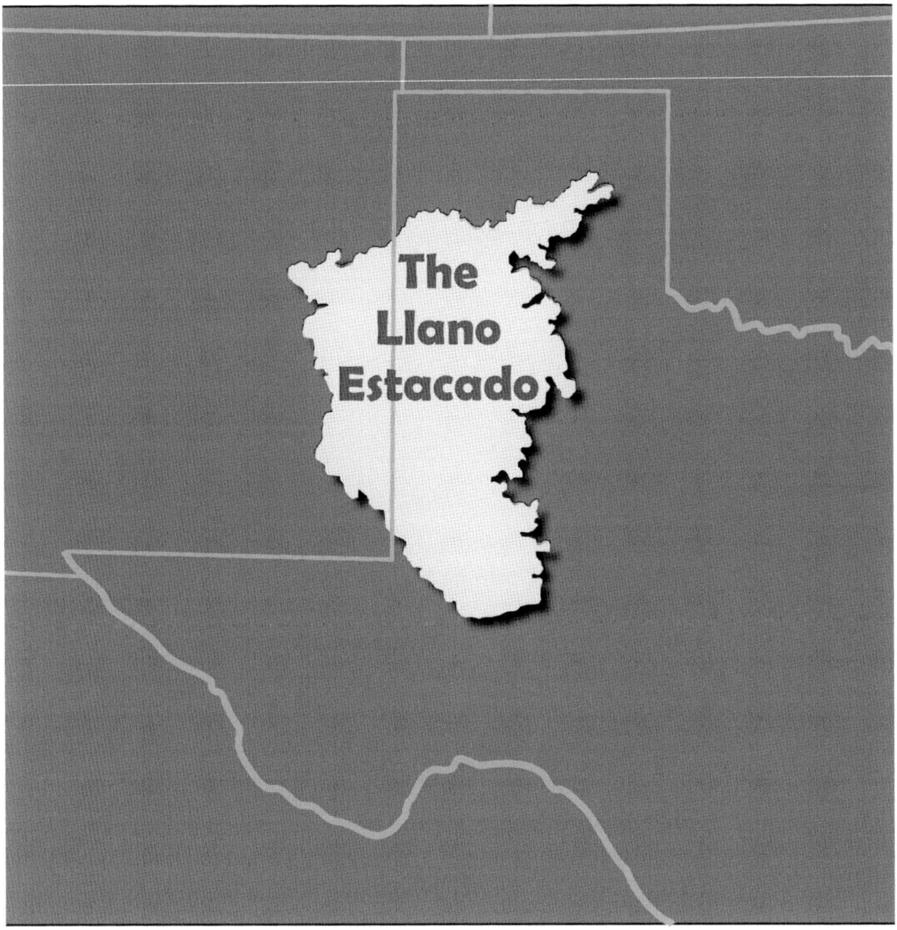

The Llano Estacado. *Map by David J. Murrah.*

in 1848, pioneers and other new arrivals, worried about Comanche control of the area and its strange environment, bypassed the Llano Estacado. Only after the U.S. Army sent thousands of troops onto the southern Great Plains in 1874 and afterward did the powerful Comanches surrender their beloved land.

During the fifty years following 1874, the Llano saw rapid development, particularly as rail lines crisscrossed the area. Coming first in the modern Anglo approach to the High Plains were cattlemen with their large, sweeping ranches. They replaced the great bison and wild mustang herds with cattle. Next, farmer-stockmen arrived, raising a few crops and some cattle, and then farmers, especially in the early 1900s after abundant rainfall essentially turned the region into a garden, crowded onto the land.

Finally, cities, such as Amarillo, Plainview, Midland and Lubbock, developed into major trade centers. Lubbock, with its road and rail networks spreading like spokes on a wheel in all directions in the very heart of the Llano, became the "Hub City" of the plains. In the 1920s and afterward, its major state college, Texas Tech, added to the sense of Lubbock as the busy "Hub" of the southern High Plains, that huge, outsized plateau stretching above the storied caprock escarpment.

All that aside, this book represents regional history—good regional history we trust. It is a collection of fifty-six brief stories, containing always interesting and lively but sometimes unfamiliar and remarkable little tales of the Llano Estacado and its eastern caprock escarpment. The accounts are concise, revealing and instructive. They are also enjoyable and user-friendly. Collectively, they reveal plenty about the region's past, its people and its colorful places. Chronologically, the "hidden histories" range from an ancient, deep past to a modern, almost contemporary present.

We received much good help and assistance in putting the book together. Monte Monroe, archivist of the Southwest Collection at Texas Tech University, provided major support with photos, ideas and conversation. Likewise, Randy Vance and his assistants, especially Caitlin Leonard, in the reference services room facilitated our efforts through suggesting photos, finding rare documents and making research a pleasant experience.

We owe a major debt of gratitude to the authors who contributed essays to this volume. They were not only cooperative and supportive but also crucial to the book's completion in a timely fashion. Likewise, we are indebted to Kevin Carlson, Diane McLaurin and Kelli McLaurin, who in the very early stages of preparing the manuscript offered technical support and unstinting aid. The enthusiasm of and encouragement from Ben Gibson at The History Press was reassuring, helpful and appreciated.

Finally, for their understanding and considerable support of our work, we are grateful to our wives, Ellen Carlson and Ann Murrah, whose self-sacrifice as we plugged along in front of our computers proved invaluable.

Paul H. Carlson, Ransom Canyon, Texas
David J. Murrah, Rockport, Texas

Part I
A Deep Past

Until recent times, humans visited the Llano Estacado sporadically or, on a couple of occasions toward the north, occupied the area but in small numbers. This region—a treeless, high flat mesa that ranges from about three thousand to four thousand feet above sea level—stretches through parts of eastern New Mexico and western Texas.

Before modern times, the Llano Estacado was rich in grass and animals, including bison, pronghorns, deer and other game large and small. It became a hunter's paradise, attracting, in turn, ancient and modern Indian peoples; early Spanish explorers, hunters and traders; Anglo bison-hide seekers; and, eventually, Anglo cattlemen, farmers and townspeople.

The tales in Part I treat this early background of the Llano Estacado's history. The section looks at some of the earliest humans to use the region, mysteries associated with the large place, explorers who traversed it and some more recent activities on it.

Chapter 1

Lubbock Area's Ancient Past

Paul H. Carlson and David J. Murrah

In our corner of West Texas, including Lubbock, history by most standard definitions is recent—"current events," some Greek, Roman and British historians might call it. Still, the history of our city and region extends a few centuries into the past, and if we consider the arrival of some of the first humans here, its archaeological record reaches back nearly twelve thousand years to Clovis and Folsom cultures.

Clovis people were among the earliest identifiable humans in our area. They were migratory hunters and foragers who concentrated on such big game animals as deer, antelope and now-extinct grazers, such as ancient, straight-horned bison and Columbian mammoths. They also hunted smaller animals, of course, and they gathered seeds, fruits, berries and nuts. In our area, their culture prevailed from approximately 11,400 years ago to 10,800 years ago—some 600 years.

Then, rather abruptly, the Clovis tradition, or at least features that identify it, faded. Most likely, as they adapted to new conditions, Clovis ways of life evolved and their societies changed.

As the Clovis culture declined, the Folsom tradition expanded, at least in our region. It dominated the period another 600 years, from approximately 10,800 years ago to 10,200 years ago. Folsom people had much in common with their Clovis predecessors: big game hunters who also took smaller animals and foraged for plants, seeds, nuts and berries. Like the Clovis, the Folsom culture after a time faded or merged into different groups and disappeared.

Reasons for the Clovis and Folsom disappearance are a matter of wonderful controversy. Some scientists argue that these early High Plains inhabitants were such efficient hunters that they killed off the very animals they needed to survive.

Others point to a changing climate. They suggest that about ten thousand years ago, as huge northern glaciers retreated at the end of the Pleistocene epoch, modern weather patterns emerged. Temperatures warmed. Streams, lakes, swamps, bogs and marshy lowlands that supported very large mammals dried up. The plains grasslands shifted from tall, coarse varieties that supported huge mammoths and straight-horned bison to a mixed prairie cover of short grasses. As a result, a great die-off of the largest grass-eating animals occurred. In turn, the demise of straight-horned bison and large mammoths placed pressure on carnivores, scavengers and other creatures ecologically dependent on the big grass eaters.

In this Pleistocene, or Ice Age, extinction, ancient horses, two genera of bison and ancient camels disappeared. Four-horned antelope, wooly and Columbian mammoths, mastodons, giant anteaters, dire wolves, tapirs, saber-tooth tigers, short-faced bears and many large rodents were

Mammoths, like these life-sized replicas at the Lubbock Lake Landmark, once roamed the Llano Estacado. *Courtesy Paul H. Carlson.*

among those that became extinct. Perhaps 66 percent of large animal species were lost.

As first the Clovis and later the Folsom cultures faded, numerous regional traditions emerged. Like their predecessors, the newer groups thrived for a period before disappearing, fading over time or merging into still other societies and cultures.

Then, several centuries later, a 2,000-year drought—the "altithermal," as it is called—brought additional changes to the natural landscape and human occupation. In the Llano Estacado area, the altithermal extended from about 6,500 years ago to about 4,500 years ago. It triggered environmental changes of enormous significance, further altering plant life, animal species and the way people of the region lived.

As time passed, human societies shifted, cultures evolved and different peoples emerged. They may have prospered for a century or more, but then they, too, moved on, faded into other groups or disappeared.

Among some of the more recent High Plains groups are people we know as Apaches and Comanches. Apaches in several divisions came at a very early date, some of them through the Great Basin country to what today is New Mexico and Arizona, but after about 1400, other divisions overran much of the region east of the Rocky Mountains.

Comanches began showing up about 1700. They traveled south through the Great Basin and then moved eastward onto the southern plains, pushing aside Apaches and other native groups over a wide area—parts of Colorado, Kansas, Oklahoma, Texas and New Mexico—a region that became known as *Comancheria*.

Beginning tentatively in the sixteenth century, Spaniards, such as Francisco Vasquez de Coronado, coming from the south challenged both native people, such as Pueblos, and the more recently arriving Apaches and Comanches. Spaniards and Indians struggled over land and resources and, in doing so, established additional societies and cultures.

The Lubbock area's modern agricultural/ranching/urban society is about 150 years old, a relatively short history when compared to the 600-year Clovis and Folsom eras. But its deep past reaches back nearly to the time when humans first arrived in our corner of North America.

Chapter 2

Arch Lake Woman

Dolores Mosser

In May 1967, Earl Green, director of the West Texas Museum at Texas Tech, was summoned to an archaeological excavation near Arch, New Mexico, located just west of the Texas state line in Roosevelt County southeast of Portales. Near Arch Lake, Professor Green, an expert in Paleoamerican geoarchaeology, found several people working a burial site of "considerable antiquity."

The urgent summons had come from James Warnica, president of the El Llano Archeology Society of Portales, New Mexico. A few days before, on May 20, society members Gregg Moore and Cecil Clark had discovered human remains on a high ridge of sand hills south of the Arch Lake—a skeleton that soon became known as Arch Lake Woman.

During the project, the archeological team took measures to ensure the remains would be properly preserved for future study. Green supervised and photographed the final excavation. The intact skeleton was of a Paleo-American woman seventeen to nineteen years of age. Eastern New Mexico University in Portales took possession of the skeleton, artifacts and project data. For nearly twenty years, Arch Lake Woman was exhibited at the university's Blackwater Draw Museum, a fascinating institution for years credited as the home of the first recovered Clovis points from twelve thousand or more years ago.

Amazingly, after the remains and grave were found in 1967, the story of the Arch Lake Woman attracted little attention, except locally. In 1990, however, archaeologists from England's Oxford University descended on eastern New Mexico to examine the skeleton. Their radiocarbon dating indicated her remains as dating from ten thousand years ago, making her the third-oldest set of human remains to be discovered in North America.

In 2000, another team led by the prominent archaeologist David Owsley from the National Museum of Natural History in Washington, D.C., came to "reexamine" Arch Lake Woman's burial history. The team utilized research methodologies unavailable forty years earlier, including geologic context, bone chemistry, AMS radiocarbon age, cultural affiliation, burial practice and associated artifact assemblage. Its investigation led to a comprehensive study of the discovery, published in 2010 as *Arch Lake Woman: Physical Anthropology and Geoarchaeology*. The book's authors dedicated their study to Dr. F. Earl Green, a native of Slaton, Texas, and acknowledged his important work in the Clovis culture of eastern New Mexico and West Texas.

From the geological data dating to 1967, the researchers first examined the burial pit. The people living with Arch Lake Woman, the researchers determined, had dug a grave with vertical walls in sand deposits three feet above the original land surface. As time passed, three different and millennial-separated phases of sand deposition had covered the grave site.

Arch Lake Woman was positioned fully prone with a bone tool lying across her ribs. In harder ground surfaces, grave diggers usually placed skeletons in a fetal position.

She was five and one-half feet tall. Her skull resembled Native Americans', and her teeth were not worn. She ate buffalo meat and plants native to the Texas Panhandle.

A stone knife and bone tool buried with her were typical Paleoamerican utensils. Around her waist was a disintegrated bag that contained pulverized ocher. After ten thousand years, the ocher powder was still "vivid" red. She also wore a necklace of nineteen drilled beads made from talc, a mineral similar to soapstone. The report placed the closest talc deposits to Arch

Stone scraping tools and talc necklace beads were buried with Arch Lake Woman. *Courtesy Dolores Mosser.*

Lake as Hembrillo Canyon in New Mexico, near Van Horn, Texas, or in the Llano uplift in central Texas. Obviously, Arch Lake Woman's people traded with Native American groups far from their Llano Estacado homeland.

Similarities to other recovered ancient North Americans included her jewelry, tools and the red ocher. Her robust arm and leg bones showed she worked hides and carried heavy loads. Her feet suggested she traveled only short distances.

Despite the new information about Arch Lake Woman, researchers were unable to determine the cause of death. As to her cultural associations, they pointed to a ten-thousand-year-old Plainview-style campsite located thirty-two miles northwest of Arch Lake as a possible home.

Arch Lake Woman, once of little scholarly interest, now holds a stellar place in the world of human science as one of the oldest Paleoamericans ever found.

This essay is from a forthcoming larger study of the Portales Valley Trail of Living Waters.

Chapter 3

The Coronado Campsite in Blanco Canyon

Jack Becker

"*We…arrived at some plains so without landmarks that it was as if we were in the middle of the sea.*" So wrote Francisco Vasquez de Coronado in a 1541 letter to his king, Charles V of Spain. Coronado was describing his first impressions of the Llano Estacado.

In all likelihood, Coronado was the first European to compare the emptiness of the landscape to the sea. Spanish explorers found the Llano so flat and disorienting that it took extraordinary efforts to keep from losing expedition members when men became separated from the group.

After crossing the plains and nearly running out of water and food, members of the huge Coronado *entrada* were in need of rest when they reached the eastern edge of the Llano. The expedition camped at the first canyon it found. But which one? Scholars continue to debate the exact route Coronado took and where he stopped after his confusing and perilous journey through eastern New Mexico and across the Llano Estacado.

Most scholars place Coronado's large campsites (there were two of them) in the eastern canyons of the Llano, locating them at places ranging from the Canadian River Valley south to the Concho River Valley. Growing evidence suggests Blanco Canyon in Crosby and Floyd Counties on the eastern edge of the Llano Estacado as the most likely site where the Coronado *entrada* stopped to rest after its long journey across the plains.

At that site, tantalizing evidence has been showing up for years, suggesting a sixteenth-century Spanish presence in and near Blanco Canyon. Bits

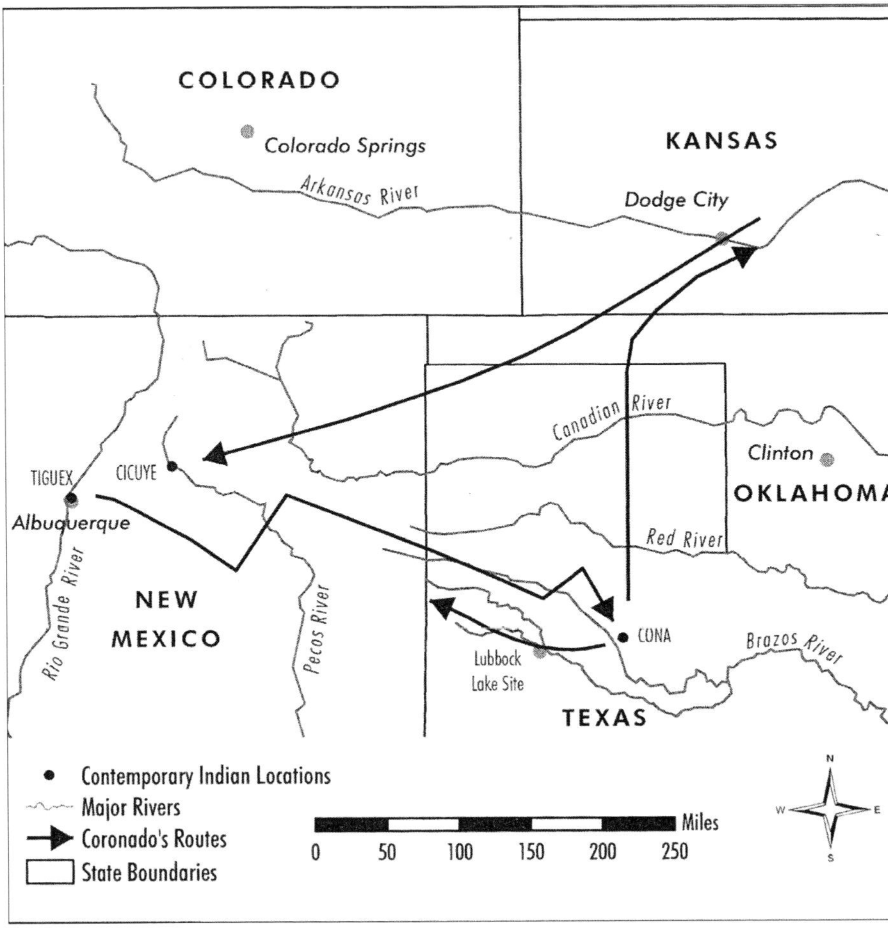

Coronado's route across the Llano Estacado. *Courtesy Matt Crawford and Donald Blakeslee.*

and pieces of Spanish armor, chainmail, crossbow points, horseshoes and fragments of horse tack have been found, all of which are known to have been used by members of the Coronado *entrada.*

Besides the physical evidence, there are letters and other written accounts that describe the campsites. Although the physical descriptions are often quite accurate, they were written some 470 years ago, and much has changed during the intervening years. Chroniclers of the expedition wrote of the second campsite as a canyon 2.6 miles wide and 26 miles long, with a stream of running water and plenty of trees for firewood, with easy access to wild game on the Llano and in the rolling hills to the east. The accounts describe

Blanco Canyon more precisely than any other canyon along the eastern edge of the Llano Estacado.

Coronado did not stay long in the first canyon. It could not supply his expedition with adequate provisions, which comprised 1,800 people and over two thousand head of livestock. The *entrada* quickly picked up and moved south, and four days later, it came to a place that good evidence suggests was Blanco Canyon. A four-day journey south to Blanco Canyon means the first canyon was more than likely Tule Canyon, less than sixty miles to the north.

One reason it is difficult to pinpoint the second Coronado campsite is the degree of change that has taken place to the land in the intervening years. Over-grazing along White River and in Blanco Canyon and agricultural irrigation on the plains have lowered the water table and destroyed vegetation to the point that Blanco Canyon is all but unrecognizable from the written reports of 470 years ago. Early pioneers wrote of the year-round water, free-flowing springs and wild plums and grapes that once grew in the canyon, none of which would describe Blanco Canyon today.

Coronado did not realize he had stumbled into an area that native peoples had used for thousands of years. Every year, native inhabitants traveled to the canyon for the same reasons Coronado stopped there: it provided easy access to the Llano and abundant natural resources, including water.

While resting in Blanco Canyon, Coronado made decisions that changed the nature of the expedition. It had become obvious that the *entrada* was too large to be supported with food and water from the surrounding semi-arid land, and Quivira, the fabled Cities of Gold he was seeking, was still some distance away.

Thus, after a bit more than two weeks in Blanco Canyon, Coronado and 50 men headed north and then east in a last vain attempt to find Quivira and its great wealth. He directed Captain Tristan de Arellano to lead the main force (about 1,700 people) back to New Mexico. On its return, the expedition may have passed through the far north side of modern Lubbock, camping for a night near the modern Lubbock Lake Historical Site before returning along either Blackwater Draw or upper Yellow House Draw.

Chapter 4

The Llano Estacado's *La Pista de Agua Viva*

Sammie Simpson and Paul H. Carlson

La Pista de Agua Viva, or the Trail of Living Water, was a Spanish phrase used from the seventeenth century to near the present day to describe important water routes across the Llano Estacado of western Texas and eastern New Mexico. Mainly, the term refers to such water courses as 1) the Canadian River Valley, 2) the Tierra Blanca Creek–Red River route through Palo Duro Canyon, 3) Running Water Draw and White River through Blanco Canyon and 4) Blackwater and Yellow House Draws that merge in modern Lubbock as part of the Upper Brazos River system.

Less often, humans used additional trails to cross the flat, featureless Llano Estacado, especially in the region's deeper past. Such routes included the upper Colorado River drainage system's Sulphur Draw and Beals Creek with its Sulphur Springs, Mackenzie, Seminole and Monument Draws. Sulphur Springs and Seminole Draws are prominent cuts in the Llano, and as late as the second half of the nineteenth century, American Indians, soldiers and others followed them, for at different places, by digging into the draws' bottoms, humans could find water.

For early Spanish and American travelers, the northern trails represented significant routes. Water and its availability, of course, were the keys to such use. The draws normally provided living water or cut close to permanent sources. Plus, *playa* lakes, the large circular depressions that often contained water, could be found in some abundance toward the north.

American Indians used *La Pista de Agua Viva* from well before Spanish explorers appeared. Apaches were using such water courses, especially in the

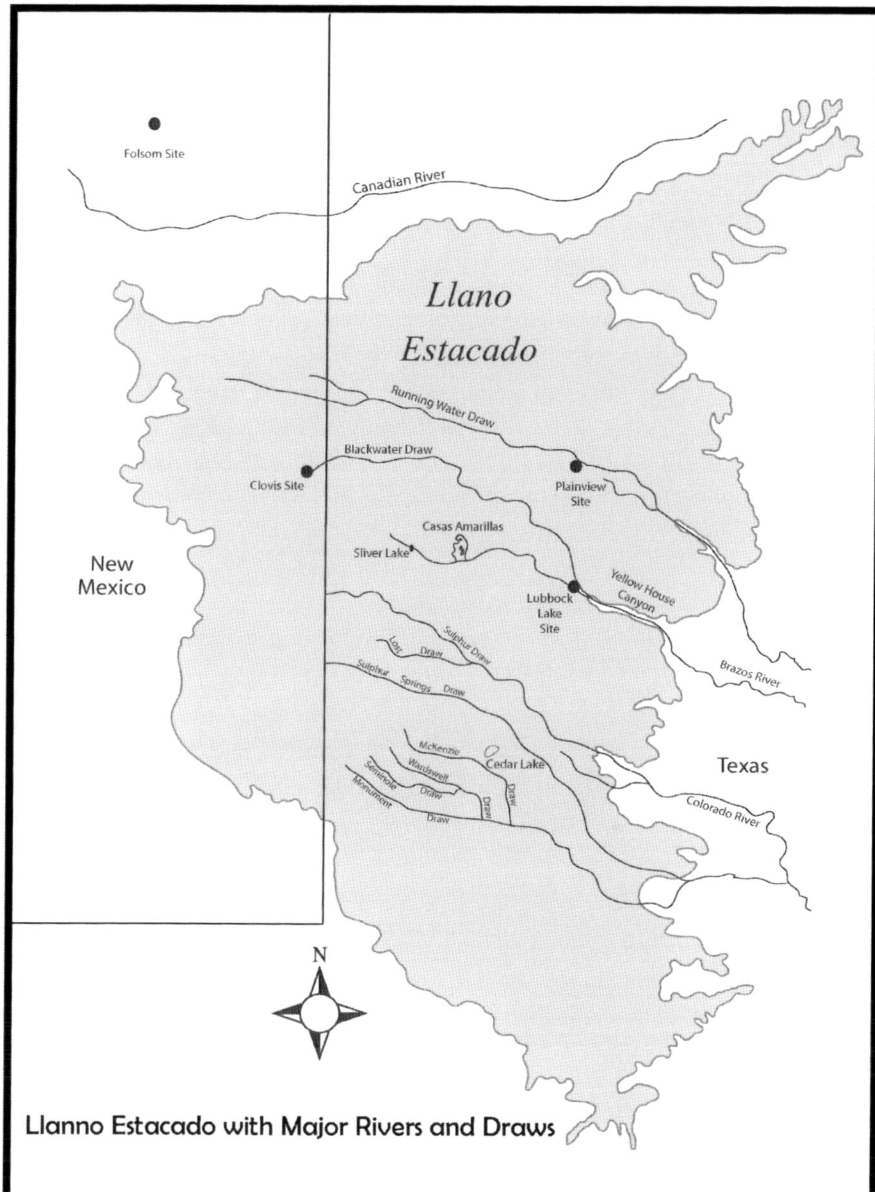

Major archaeological sites and water courses across the Llano Estacado. *Courtesy Curtis Peoples.*

southern sections, until the mid- to late nineteenth century. As they entered the region in the eighteenth century, Comanches followed well-worn trails through the high tableland.

After a 1786 treaty between Comanches and Spaniards, comancheros (traders from New Mexico villages) and *ciboleros* (bison hunters) followed the familiar northern routes from New Mexico onto and across the Llano Estacado.

Comanchero trading sites existed in most of the canyons on the eastern side of the Llano. The colorful traders also maintained such sites in *Casas Amarillas*, along Yellow House Draw, and near Muchaque Peak on the divide between the Colorado and Brazos Rivers in modern Borden County.

Comancheros continued to ply their trade along routes of *La Pista de Agua Viva* until well after Comanches, Cheyennes and Kiowas moved onto reservations and began receiving goods from the federal government.

But Spanish explorers had followed *La Pista de Agua Viva* long before comancheros or *ciboleros*. Francisco Coronado in 1541 was the first when he crossed from New Mexico to Blanco Canyon.

Some scholars suggest that Spanish Christian missionaries in the 1630s and afterward crossed the Llano along one of the water courses to administer spiritual needs to Jumano groups in the modern Ballinger–San Angelo–Menard area. With greater certainty, Spanish military officers Jose Mares in 1787–88 and an aging Francisco Amangual in 1808 used *La Pista de Agua Viva* as they searched for shorter routes between San Antonio and Santa Fe.

Americans likewise followed *La Pista de Agua Viva* when they hazarded a crossing of the High Plains. Such crossings included the 1841 Texan–Santa Fe Expedition, an ill-fated effort to establish the jurisdiction of Texas over eastern New Mexico.

Captain Randolph B. Marcy of the United States Army crossed and recrossed the Llano Estacado along different routes in 1849, and in 1852, he examined the headstreams of the Red River. In 1856, he explored the upper Brazos River through modern Lubbock.

In 1855, Captain John Pope, later to win fame in the Civil War, visited the Llano in its southern reaches, and Colonel Ranald Mackenzie of the army in 1872 crossed the northern portions to Forts Sumner and Bascom in New Mexico.

Such activity suggests that routes of *La Pista de Agua Viva* were busy. In 1832, for example, Bill Williams, an ornery and grizzled old mountain man, and Albert Pike, an adventure-loving Yankee who during the Civil War became a Confederate diplomat, led a party of forty-five fur trappers eastward from New Mexico down Blackwater Draw and *Canyon del Rescate* (Ransom Canyon) to the rolling plains below the Llano Estacado. They had little success in finding beaver dams, but the upper Blackwater route they followed spread some fourteen horse trails wide.

Clearly, routes of *La Pista de Agua Viva* provided water necessary for traversing the grass-dominated but often desert-like Llano Estacado. Over time, some of the trails became wide and well marked. *La Pista de Agua Viva*, as its name implies, was for centuries an indispensable trail of living water.

Chapter 5

The Lady in Blue

Paul H. Carlson

Maria de Jesus de Agreda (1602–1665), the Lady in Blue, was born and reared in Agreda, Spain, became a Franciscan nun and, in 1620, entered a convent in her village. The convent had once been her father's residence, and a few years later, Sister Maria became the convent's abbess. As a Franciscan, she wore a habit colored brown with an outer cloak of coarse blue cloth, and thus became known as the "Lady in Blue."

Maria de Agreda was a mystic who in the 1620s often lapsed into deep trances during which she said she made spiritual journeys to North America, including Spanish West Texas. During her transmigrations, Maria administered to Jumanos especially but to other native groups as well, preaching the benefits of Christianity. Her bilocations occurred as often as four times in a twenty-four-hour period, and years later, she claimed to have visited North America five hundred times.

After Maria reported her visitations to her confessor, Fray Sebastian Marcilla of Agreda, news of her unusual activities spread, including to Mexico in 1628 and then to New Mexico. By making inquiries and seeking news about the young Franciscan, church leaders in New Mexico sought to provide information about the mysterious nun in their region.

At the same time, Jumanos from Texas showed up in New Mexico claiming that a woman dressed in blue similar to a painting of Mother Luisa de Carrion in Mission San Antonio in Isleta, south of Albuquerque, had come among them and spoken to them in their own tongue. The Jumanos asked for religious teachers for themselves and their neighbors.

The Lady in Blue, María de Jesús de Ágreda, age twenty. Painting in the Museum of the Viceroyalty of New Spain, Tepotzotlán, Mexico. *www.mariadeagreda.info.*

In response, Franciscans Juan de Salas and Diego Lopez, with Jumanos as their guides, went looking for the Lady in Blue. They traveled eastward from Santa Fe in 1629, seeking her in the upper Colorado River region—in the modern Ballinger–San Angelo–Menard area. Fray Juan searched again in 1632, and this time one of the mission fathers with him stayed among the Jumanos for six months.

Perhaps what the Jumanos really wanted was Spanish protection from Apaches and native tribes to their east. In addition, Jumanos, who for years had been developing trade relations with Spaniards, wanted to keep exchange routes open to New Mexico and at the same time get the Europeans to secure and maintain Jumano access to hunting grounds on the High Plains—the Llano Estacado.

In subsequent years, additional Spanish missionaries sought the enigmatic Lady in Blue as they proselytized among the Jumanos. But no permanent relationships—either trade or religious—developed, and Jumanos, in the face of Apache attacks, continued to struggle and recede.

In Spain, meanwhile, Alonso de Benavides, who had been to New Mexico and had heard the Lady in Blue stories, found Sister Maria de Agreda. He discovered her in her convent at Agreda in Castile Province near the Ebro River in northern Spain. In 1631, Benavides convinced Maria to write a letter explaining her visions and her "visits" to North America. In the letter, she wrote that the spiritual journeys had begun in 1620, when she was eighteen years old and had first entered the convent. Her visitations, she said, ended in 1631.

Maria's letter went to New Mexico. Here, it inspired additional efforts, such as the second expedition of Juan de Salas to find the Lady in Blue. The letter appeared in French, English and Dutch editions. It made Maria de Agreda famous—"one of the most eminent women in Spain"—for a time. For twenty-two years, she corresponded with Spanish

King Philip IV, becoming something of a spiritual advisor and confidant to the political leader.

Eventually, Maria publicly burned a copy of the letter and disavowed the experiences it purported to describe.

Nonetheless, Maria de Jesus de Agreda was a very serious abbess. She made her convent of Immaculate Conception successful and led it in serving people in northeast Spain. Sister Maria was a prolific author who produced books, letters and other writings.

Maria's bilocation story remains another of those wonderful mysteries of historic West Texas.

Chapter 6

Comancheros

Paul H. Carlson and Randy Vance

Comancheros were Hispanic and mixed-blood New Mexican and Pueblo traders, some from "indigent and rude classes" and some "avid traders from time immemorial," wrote Josiah Gregg. Charles Kenner wrote that Americans viewed the "striking and picturesque" New Mexicans at first as "harmless rovers" but later as "notorious villains."

Comancheros—the name first appeared in print in 1843—carried craft goods, foodstuffs and other articles to the plains and exchanged them with Comanches and other native peoples for bison robes and hides, cattle, meat and sometimes humans. Tobacco, sugar, flour, corn, bread, cloth, guns, lead, iron arrow and spear points and liquor were also part of the commerce.

After 1706, when Comanches first showed up at Taos, trade between the tribe and New Mexico's villagers increased. But at the same time, New Mexicans suffered from increasingly frequent Comanche raids. To put an end to the raiding, Juan Bautista de Anza, the governor of New Mexico, with a huge force struck a large Comanche village in 1779, killed its chief (Cuerno Verde) and dealt a severe blow to Comanche power and influence. Over the next half dozen years, various other Comanche leaders accepted peace.

Then, in 1786, at Pecos Pueblo in eastern New Mexico, Governor Anza and Ecueracapa, an important Comanche spokesman, agreed to a broad treaty of peace and friendship. The Pecos Treaty, as it was called, "opened the way for the full development of the trade." Prior to the treaty, commerce had been limited mainly to trade fairs at Taos, Pecos Pueblo and various Spanish settlements.

A Comanchero home and cart in New Mexico. *Sketch from* Panhandle Pilgrimage *by Pauline and R.L. Robertson.*

After the treaty, comanchero trading grew and flourished. With items on pack animals or in large two-wheeled carts, comancheros traveled a couple of times a year to favorite spots and awaited their native trade partners.

The Canadian River Valley, the upper Red River with its various tributaries, Running Water Draw and Blanco Canyon, Black Water and Yellow House Draws and several tributaries of the upper Colorado River contained trading sites. One trading site existed as far east as the juncture of Duck Creek and the Brazos River in modern Kent County. According to a U.S. Army recognizance officer, in 1870, some six hundred Indians camped there along an old "Mexican cart road"—a comanchero trail.

The *Casas Amarillas* basin southwest of present-day Littlefield near the upper Yellow House Draw was a popular rendezvous. Traders built a small stone shelter on a bluff overlooking the large basin.

Muchaque Peak, southeast of modern Gail on the upland between the Brazos and Colorado Rivers, was also a favorite meeting spot. To the spot, Comanches and others brought cattle taken from ranches to the southeast and exchanged them for comanchero goods.

In today's Ransom Canyon (*Canon Rescata*) east of Lubbock, bartering also appeared. Here, traffic in humans may have become part of the exchange, although Indians probably interpreted *Canon Rescata* as "trader's canyon," and we are uncertain how often the swap of humans occurred. It is probably exaggerated.

Sometime late in the colorful trade's existence, comancheros contracted with New Mexican businessmen. Texans usually identified them as "German Jews." Charles Probst and August Kirchner were "immigrant beef contractors from Prussia" who bought cattle from comancheros. The businessmen, in turn, sold the cattle in northern markets. William Rosenthal also dealt with comancheros for cattle.

Businessmen in Las Vegas, Santa Fe and Taos sometimes staked the comancheros, providing them with manufactured goods, foodstuffs, cloth and other items to exchange with Comanches for cattle, horses, hides and robes.

In the 1870s, the comanchero trade declined. Comanches had agreed in an 1867 treaty to settle on reservations in Indian Territory (Oklahoma) in exchange for food, clothes, cloth, tools and other items from the U.S. government. At least one Comanche band was not privy to the treaty and continued to deal with the dwindling number of comancheros. Others left the reservation to hunt and trade—and sometimes to raid Texas ranches for livestock. Then, after 1874–75, when the Red River War in the Panhandle closed down Comanche opportunities for hunting and trading, comanchero traffic withered and died.

Some comancheros, such as Polonio Ortiz, became guides for the U.S. Army. Some, such as Casimero Romero, became sheepherders or *pastores*, with headquarters along the upper Canadian River.

The comanchero market was always in flux. American traders impacted the commerce. Indian populations declined. Cattle became a major focus of the enterprise. Gun-running and alcohol use increased in volume. Despite the changes, comanchero activity in West Texas existed for nearly a century.

Chapter 7

The Mackenzie Trail

Paul H. Carlson

There is more than one "Mackenzie Trail." But as described by the late Texas Tech University historian Ernest Wallace, the significant Mackenzie Trail extended from near Fort Griffin north of Albany in Shackelford County westward to the mouth of Blanco Canyon in Crosby and Floyd Counties. In the early 1870s, it became a major military road.

Ranald S. Mackenzie, for whom the trail is named, was a West Point graduate (head of his class), a Civil War veteran (Federal troops) and a highly competent army officer (Fourth Cavalry) in the American West, especially Texas. Tributes to his role in the settlement of West Texas abound. Mackenzie Park and Mackenzie Middle School in Lubbock are named for Colonel Mackenzie, as is Mackenzie Mountain, an upland with two caprocked mesas joined by a saddle and located along the Kent-Scurry County line about forty miles north of Snyder. Mackenzie Reservoir near Silverton is also named for him. In addition, there are two prominent markers that recognize Mackenzie and his road. One is near its beginning, just north of Stamford; the other is on the courthouse square at Plainview.

The Mackenzie Trail developed in 1871 after military officials ordered Mackenzie to move against Comanche warriors in western Texas. Accordingly, Colonel Mackenzie collected supplies, wagons, pack mules, scouts and his troops at old Camp Cooper in Throckmorton County, five miles north of Fort Griffin.

Here, the trail began. It proceeded west to cross the Clear Fork of the Brazos River near the southern corner of Throckmorton and

Haskell Counties. It forded California Creek in the northwest corner of Jones County, and maintaining the same westward direction, it crossed Oteys or Paint Creek near the Jones-Haskell County line. It passed on the north side of present Stamford and ran west along approximately the thirty-third parallel. At a point in southeastern Stonewall County, the trail veered to the northwest to traverse the Double Mountain Fork of the Brazos almost directly north of modern Hamlin. It stayed along the northwest course and passed by Cottonwood Springs between Double Mountain and modern Aspermont in a marshy wetland. From here, the trail moved up Salt Creek northwestward to cross the Salt Fork (Main Fork) of the Brazos in western Stonewall County, southwest of the present town of Peacock. Continuing toward the northwest, the route again struck the Salt Fork, this time near present Jayton, and followed the river to Duck Creek in Dickens County. The trail advanced up Duck Creek several miles and then cut abruptly northwestward again to the Freshwater Fork of the Brazos and the mouth of Blanco Canyon north of present White River Lake. Here it ended.

Ranald Slidell Mackenzie, 1876. *From* Ranald S. Mackenzie on the Texas Frontier *by Ernest Wallace.*

An old military map labeled the route between the mouth of Duck Creek and mouth of Blanco Canyon as "Mexican Cart Trail," apparently referring to two-wheeled carts (and traders from New Mexico).

Major military supply camps existed near the mouth of Duck Creek and along the Freshwater Fork of the Brazos below the mouth of Blanco Canyon. Colonel Mackenzie used the Freshwater Fork camps in 1871, 1872 and 1874. On military maps, one of the camps became known as Anderson's Fort and two of them as Supply Camp.

The Duck Creek campsite had been used for generations. In 1870, Captain Wirt Davis of the Fourth Cavalry reported the place had been occupied by between six and eight hundred Indians just prior to his arrival. Second Lieutenant Robert Carter, Mackenzie's adjutant, later wrote about

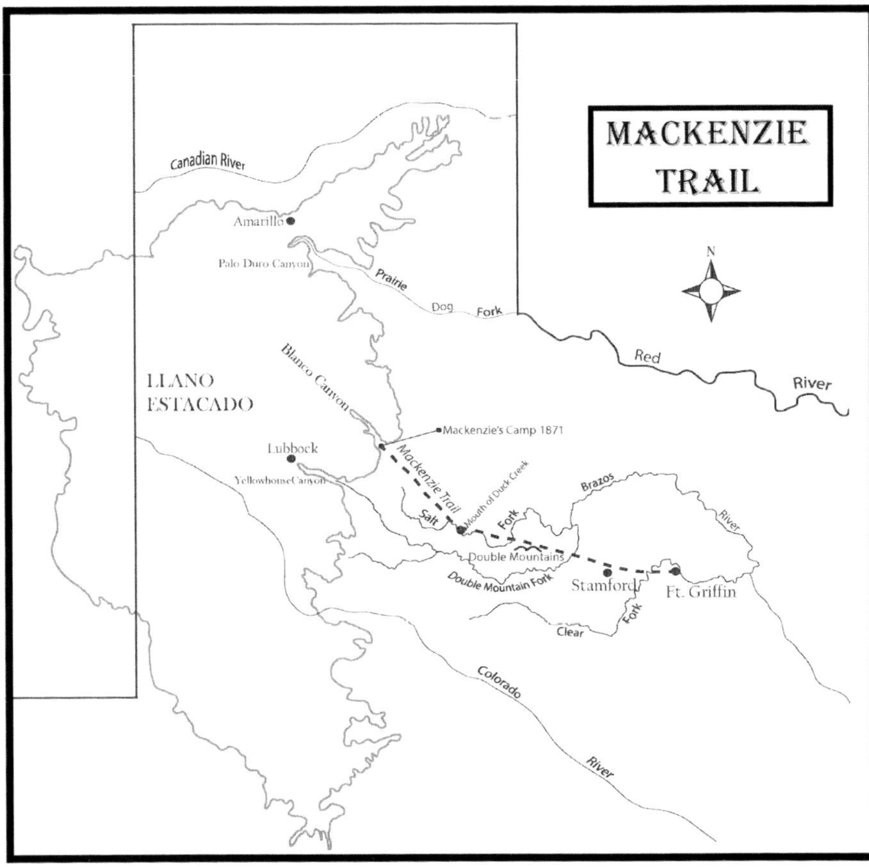

The Mackenzie Trail from Fort Richardson to Blanco Canyon in 1873. *Courtesy Curtis Peoples.*

"abandoned trading stations" in the cliff banks along Duck Creek and signs of Indian occupation.

In the 1870s, Anglo civilians used the Mackenzie Trail. Bison hunters hauled hides along it. Henry C. "Hank" Smith followed it to Blanco Canyon in 1876 and 1877. Surveyors, seeking land for early-day developers, worked part of it to reach the modern Lubbock and Yellow House Canyon area in 1877. Also in 1877, a family from Erath County on their way to New Mexico rode the trail.

There were other trails that bore Mackenzie's name. The late Bob Burton described one that ran north from Fort Concho at San Angelo to Blanco Canyon. An old military map shows one reaching in a straight line from Blanco Canyon north to old Mobeetie and Fort Elliott in the Texas Panhandle.

In 1872, Mackenzie with his Fourth Cavalry crossed the Llano Estacado from Blanco Canyon. His route became a Mackenzie Trail. It followed an old Indian road up Blanco Canyon a few miles before climbing out of the canyon on the west side. From there, it passed near modern Abernathy, reached Blackwater Draw and followed the draw to New Mexico and Fort Sumner.

Chapter 8

Quanah Parker's Birthplace

Paul H. Carlson

Scholars know when and where Quanah Parker died: at his home near Cache, Oklahoma, on February 23, 1911. However, they know little about where or when he was born, although various Quanah enthusiasts have claimed their own community as the place of his birth.

His mother was the famous Cynthia Ann Parker, or Nadauh, as her Comanche family and friends called her. His father, nearly everyone says, was Peta Nocona, a warrior of some distinction but not a chief. According to U.S. Army interpreter Horace Jones, who knew him, Nocona "was not even a 'big man' among the Comanches." Comanches captured Cynthia Ann in 1836 when she was nine years old. She probably became a "chore wife" of Nocona about five or six years later, suggesting perhaps that Quanah was born between 1843 and 1845.

Many histories and biographies, including the influential *New Handbook of Texas*, suggest Quanah was born in or near the Wichita Mountains in southwestern Oklahoma. The mountains, a series of rocky promontories and round hills, trended northwest–southeast close to the heart of what became the Comanche-Kiowa reservation.

Quanah himself suggested a different birthplace: near Cedar Lake in modern Gaines County, Texas. The large, shallow, alkali-filled lake is east–northeast of Seminole and west–northwest of Lamesa and sits in a depression between Sulphur Springs Draw and Mackenzie Draw, ancient water routes across the Llano Estacado that Indians had used for centuries. The region is ranching country dominated by oil wells and ubiquitous mesquite trees.

Quanah Parker, Comanche chief. *Courtesy Southwest Collection, Texas Tech University.*

County Road 1066 runs along the lake's northern edge near its junction with County Road 1067.

In 1907, according to Walter Posey, who later became an influential banker and local political leader, Quanah and a few Comanche friends came through Lubbock in a large new touring car. His stop in the little town of seven hundred or so people, with its unpaved streets and wooden buildings surrounding the county courthouse, attracted plenty of local attention. Lubbock citizens, including Posey, spoke with the Comanches. The Indians wanted food and water. They also needed gasoline for their automobile before continuing the fifty or so miles south to their destination.

Posey never forgot the vivid experience. Years later in interviews first with J. Evetts Haley and William C. Holden, major historians of West Texas, and subsequently with Seymour V. Connor of Texas Tech University's history department, he spoke about the Quanah visit. Posey said Quanah indicated that he was on his way to Cedar Lake. In their brief conversation, he said, Quanah mentioned there was a tradition that when possible Comanches should visit or revisit their birthplace before they died, and Quanah, now probably in his early sixties, was on his way to the locale in Gaines County.

On the northeast edge of Cedar Lake, a granite historical marker suggests the general place of Quanah's birth. In 1936, as part of its centennial celebration, the State of Texas erected the marker. It reads: "Cedar Lake, or Laguna Sabinas. Largest Alkali Lake on Plains; old Indian camp and burial site; birthplace of Quanah Parker. A skirmish between Indians and United States Cavalry under command of Lieutenant John L. Bullis took place here in October, 1875."

Quanah, whose name has been interpreted in unflattering ways, was about fifteen years old when federal troops captured his mother and baby sister Topsannah in 1860. Her capture pretty much left him and his younger brother Pecos with only modest family support. But with aid from their father and his additional wives, their uncles and others, the brothers grew to adulthood. Indeed, Quanah became a leading figure among the Comanches, first in resistance to Anglo encroachment and settlement in their land and later in the tribe's adjustment to living on their reservation.

Biographer Brian Hosmer suggests that Quanah moved from being a nomadic "hunter of the Llano Estacado" to a "cattle rancher, entrepreneur, and friend of American presidents." Once on the reservation, he adopted his mother's family name and became Quanah Parker.

Quanah spoke fluently both the Comanche language and the Indian "sign language." Although he spoke English haltingly, he did not learn how to read or write in the language. He was, like all Comanches of his day, a superb horseman. He became a powerful leader.

On the reservation, Quanah Parker was a man of two worlds. While retaining many of his Indian modes and customs, he easily converted to Anglo ways of life. Also a shrewd investor, he became a wealthy man (one of the wealthiest Indians in America) but retained his seven Comanche wives and built a twenty-two-room house to accommodate them. A business associate of several Texas ranchers, he became a friend of U.S. president Theodore Roosevelt, but upon his death, Quanah was buried in full Comanche regalia.

For all that, scholars still do not know Quanah Parker's birthplace. Nearly all Oklahoma Parkers (Peta Nocona's relatives) claim the Wichita Mountains site. Most Texas Parkers (Cynthia Ann's relatives) argue for the Cedar Lake site.

Part II
Ranches and Roads

The years 1870 to 1875, the last five of Comanche occupation of the Llano Estacado, proved to be adventurous times as bison hunters, the military and land survey crews pushed into the region. The intrusion brought conflict, resulting in the U.S. Army's intervention to force the Comanches to their reservation in Oklahoma. When Quanah Parker and his band abandoned the Llano Estacado in the summer of 1875, others were ready to occupy the region.

Sheepherders had already drifted into canyons of the Llano even before the Comanches had departed. Then, bison hunters came from Dodge City and Rath City to begin the slaughter of the huge southern herd. On their heels came cattlemen moving in from all directions, led by Charles Goodnight, who established the JA Ranch in Palo Duro Canyon in 1876. Within ten years, much of the Llano Estacado had been claimed by large cattle operations, such as the Matador, the Slaughter brothers, the IOA and the three-million-acre XIT Ranch.

The big ranches controlled the Llano for more than twenty years. However, a prolonged drought in the 1890s and a national depression began to force cattlemen to sell out. By that time, major railroads had penetrated the area. The Texas and Pacific built across the south end of the plains, establishing Colorado City, Big Spring and Midland. And at the confluence of Fort Worth and Denver and Santa Fe on the north side, Amarillo sprang up to eventually become a major city.

In 1890, Lubbock was established, but the little village remained isolated for nearly twenty years, bypassed by the railroads and the Great Western Cattle Trail. It would eventually become the "capital of the Llano Estacado," especially in the minds of German readers of the novelist Karl May, as you will learn in Part IV.

Chapter 9

Sheepherders on the Llano

Paul H. Carlson

Immediately after American soldiers defeated southern plains Indians in the Red River War of 1874–75, sheepherders pushed their ovine flocks onto the Llano Estacado. And perhaps they did it before then, for Antonio Baca claimed to have grazed sheep in the present-day Oklahoma Panhandle prior to the Civil War.

After the Red River War, former comancheros, traders from New Mexico, led the way. They knew the Llano and its rich grasslands, its life-sustaining water courses and its sheltering canyons. Many former comancheros remained friends with, or old business partners of, Comanches, Kiowas and Cheyennes. Thus, fear of an Indian attack did not inhibit them in their new pastoral enterprises.

The best known of the New Mexico sheepmen, or *pastores*, as they were called, to climb onto the Texas High Plains was Casimero Romero. In 1876, he led twelve men and their families down the Canadian River from New Mexico's Mora County to about where Tascosa and modern Boys Ranch in Potter County exist.

Romero and the others herded at least 4,500 sheep to the site. In wagons, they brought household supplies and ranching equipment to establish permanent dwellings in the area, and they drove horses and enough cattle to provide beef and milk for the settlers. They built homes of adobe and settled in to graze their sheep on the highlands—the Llano Estacado—above the river valley.

Other New Mexicans soon heard of abundant grasslands, clear springs and permanent creeks in the wide valley. They arrived with thousands of additional sheep.

Not all who came were Hispanic or Pueblo. Henry Kimball, a blacksmith, moved his sheep to a site along Rita Blanca Creek on the north side of the Canadian River. Englishmen Jim Campbell and A.B. Ledgard established a sheep ranch northwest of Rita Blanca Creek. Their flock numbered about twenty-five thousand animals. In the Lubbock area, Zachary T. Williams, a twenty-nine-year-old from Mississippi, grazed his flocks near modern Buffalo Springs Lake. He claimed to have been there as early as 1877. Richard Wilkerson, a twenty-six-year-old from Indiana, grazed sheep in Blackwater Draw in the vicinity of present-day Lubbock Country Club. John Coleman ran a very large spread across what is today Mackenzie Park. One of his five herders was Andrew Gonzales, a native of Monterrey, Mexico, and one of the first permanent Mexican-American settlers in Lubbock.

Grazing circuits extended on the Llano from north of the Canadian River south to Tule and Quitaque Canyons and beyond into the upper Brazos River drainage system west of Lubbock.

Jesus Perea, for example, herded his flocks of thirty thousand sheep to Tahoka Lake, Yellow House Canyon and Blanco Canyon. Because of the great amount of grazing land and water needed for so many sheep, Perea scattered his animals widely and took them wherever good grass and water could be found.

As the South Plains filled with sheep operations, grazing circuits became more and more fixed. As a result, some *pastores* built rough stone corrals on the open range or in the Llano's canyons to shelter themselves and their sheep.

In far upper Yellow House Draw between Silver Lake and modern Enochs—in the boundary area between Cochran, Hockley and Bailey Counties—the draw cuts a deep, wide swath (a canyon) for about three-quarters of a mile. In it, several caves pockmark the steep walls and probably provided shelter for herders. A whole series of rock fences or corrals held sheep in the little canyon. It may have been a place to hold and sort sheep during spring shearing season, but the presence of rock corrals and fences suggests permanent or semi-permanent residence.

Such was clearly the case for *pastores* in the Canadian River Valley. When the herders returned to the valley from the Llano, they settled into their adobe homes for the winter and bedded their flocks inside stone corrals. Many sheepherders on the Llano Estacado were "free grazers"

Rock and stone fences dating to the nineteenth century can be found in the upper Yellow House Draw west of Lubbock. *Courtesy Paul H. Carlson.*

who moved their flocks from New Mexico onto the plains in the spring and back again in the fall. Both settled sheepmen and cattle raisers disliked such "drifters," for too often their sheep carried communicable diseases, such as scabies.

Nonetheless, in 1880, nearly four hundred *pastores* and other sheepmen grazed perhaps 108,000 sheep in the Texas Panhandle.

By then, cattlemen had arrived, and they began to force out or buy out many of the *pastores*. Likewise, across the Llano's South Plains after 1880, ranchers and their cowboys brought in huge herds of cattle. Ten years later, in 1890, only ten thousand sheep remained in the entire Texas Panhandle. Cattle ranchers grazed most of them.

On the South Plains after 1890, only scattered farmer-ranchers, such as Hank Smith in Blanco Canyon, kept sheep. The practice of raising sheep in the state had moved elsewhere.

Chapter 10

Rath City

Cheryl Lewis and Paul H. Carlson

Rath City, located in modern Stonewall County near the Double Mountain Fork of the Brazos River, enjoyed only a short existence during the last years of bison hunting activity in Texas.

Established in December 1876, the rough-edged trade center experienced its busiest activity during the winter of 1877–78, when tens of thousands of hides were sold there. Hunter turned writer Frank Collinson reported seeing 1,100,000 hides in Rath City that hunting season. The number is an exaggeration, but Rath City hide buyers conducted at least $1 million worth of business through the 1877–78 winter.

Some four thousand bison hunters, skinners, teamsters, hide buyers and others worked the West Texas bison herds between 1876 and 1879. Many of them came to Rath City on a regular basis to sell their hides, purchase supplies and take in what few amusements that existed. The place attracted gamblers, prostitutes, transients, a Swiss count and political refugee and cowboys to its saloons and dance hall. The entertainment has been called "brutally raw," and such later famous individuals as Pat Garrett and Elliott B. Roosevelt were there.

Charles Rath, a Dodge City–based businessman and hide buyer, was largely responsible for Rath City, a place that some hunters and teamsters called either "Rath's Store" or "Camp Reynolds." Rath, who had a store at Adobe Walls in 1874 when Comanches and Cheyennes struck the Texas Panhandle trade center, had determined to move south and get below the bison herds that still remained in Texas.

Remains of a building that once stood at Rath City. *Courtesy Cheryl Lewis.*

If local lore is correct, the forty-year-old Rath, sitting on horseback with a compass in his hand, led a large wagon train from Fort Elliott in the Panhandle due south. Behind him in the first wagon rode men with picks, shovels and other equipment to cut a passable road down creek and riverbanks and through draws and arroyos to a town site Rath planned to lay out. The trail that Charles Rath and the others carved out in the fall of 1876 essentially followed what is today U.S. Highway 83. It passed through modern Wheeler, Collingsworth, Childress, Cottle, King and Stonewall Counties.

Following the first wagon came bison hunters and skinners, teamsters, saloon operators, a laundryman, traders, storekeepers and others—about fifty to sixty people in all. Many of the oxen-drawn wagons hauled bars of lead, kegs of gunpowder and whiskey, boxes of tobacco and other trade items the hunters might want. One wagon, or so the story goes, carried several women who planned to operate a dance hall.

In December 1876, after several weeks on the trail, the men laid out Rath City. Using native stone for foundations, men constructed wood-frame buildings using sod for walls and bison hides as covers. Some buildings were only tents. The place held a couple of saloons, the dance hall, Rath's large store, a blacksmith shop, a barbershop, a laundry, a combination restaurant-hotel, a wagon yard and sod corrals to hold horses, mules and oxen.

In the spring and summer of 1878, with bison herds having been depleted, Rath City declined, and by the late spring of 1879, it had been deserted. All that remains visible at the site are the graves of bison hunters Spotted Jack, disgruntled Tom Lumpkin and an unnamed person.

Today, the site, located about eight miles north of Hamlin just off Highway 83, lies beneath a wheat field. In the past dozen years, archaeologists after the annual harvest have dug through the abandoned site to find old foundations and other evidence of Rath City's material culture.

Rath City boomed for a couple of years in the late 1870s, but like the larger bison hide business, it declined as quickly as the disappearance of the magnificent-looking brown beasts that had given both the venture and the village a reason to exist.

Chapter 11

The XIT Ranch Windmill

David J. Murrah

For a half century, the giant XIT Ranch windmill stood as one of the tallest structures ever built on the Llano Estacado. Created out of great necessity to convert wind to water, it rose 132 feet, reaching above the rim of Yellow House Canyon to catch the West Texas wind. For its day, it was an engineering marvel and was reportedly the tallest windmill in the world.

The windmill, constructed by the fabled XIT Ranch about 1887, stood at the Yellow House Division headquarters sixteen miles north of Levelland. It was one of 325 windmills spread over the ranch's three million acres that extended two hundred miles north to the top of the Panhandle.

Established in 1885 by the Capitol Freehold Land and Investment Company of Chicago on the land it received in exchange for building a new capitol in Austin, the XIT at the time was the largest fenced ranch in the world. Ranch owners quickly stocked their property with 150,000 head of cattle.

XIT officials soon discovered they did not have enough surface water for the animals, especially during an extended drought that became acute in 1886. As a result, the ranch invested heavily in water wells and windmills.

The site of the tall windmill was a spring at the base of a modest one-hundred-foot bluff in *Casas Amarillas* (Yellow Houses), a major landmark in the area. Shallow caves just below the bluff's rim gave the place its distinctive name, because from a distance, they could look like a complex of Indian dwellings. The XIT made *Casas Amarillas* its breeding pasture for the sprawling ranch. The spring could not provide enough water for the

The XIT Ranch, world's tallest windmill, circa 1910. *From* Hockley County: The First Fifty Years, 1921–1971 *by Lillian Brasher.*

hundreds of cows driven to the deep basin, and the high bluff blocked the wind. The remedy was to erect a high wooden tower, one taller than any ever attempted. Built of timbers freighted to the ranch by wagon from a railhead 150 miles away, the structure boosted the huge sixteen-foot-diameter wheel sufficiently far above the bluff to catch the wind.

To service its many windmills, the XIT employed two full-time windmill men for each of its seven divisions. The windmill mechanisms required frequent attention, including regular lubrication. Climbing the standard thirty-two-foot towers was bad enough, but scaling the high tower at the Yellow House made the job even more difficult, especially during windy days. One windmiller fell to his death from the high tower, and after that, the ranch had difficulty finding someone to work on it. Another had started up the tower, but as he got higher and his footing became shakier, he thought the tower was falling, causing him to jump into the windmill's stock tank.

In 1901, XIT owners sold the Yellow House division to Austin banker and cattleman George W. Littlefield, who a decade later began selling land to prospective farmers and established the town of Littlefield.

In 1923, much of the remainder of the ranch was sold to the Yellow House Land Company, which, in turn, established the communities of Pep and Whitharral.

In the summer of 1926, a Boy Scout troop made the sixteen-mile hike from Levelland to the *Casas Amarillas* basin. There stood the tall windmill, the equivalent of a thirteen-story building. One of the scouts, sixteen-year-old LeRoy Murrah, decided to climb it, but when he got halfway up, he said it was steadily shaking, and he decided to go no farther. It proved a wise decision, for on Thanksgiving Day that fall of 1926, in the midst of a raging sandstorm, the tower toppled.

At the time the windmill fell, the disposition of the three million acres of the old XIT was nearly complete. Today, ninety thousand people live on what was once the big ranch. They live on farms, on ranches and in such communities as Littlefield, Friona, Muleshoe, Farwell, Bovina, Texline and Channing.

Two million of its acres are now in cultivation, producing cotton, wheat, grain sorghum, corn and other crops. The other million acres remain in grass, mostly in the northwestern corner of the Panhandle and along the Canadian River.

In Texas, two towering tributes to the old XIT remain. One is the 311-foot-tall state capitol in Austin, built in exchange for the land. The other is a 114-foot replica of the Yellow House windmill, constructed in 1969 by the citizens of Littlefield.

Chapter 12

Great Western Trail: The Almost Forgotten Last Major Texas Cattle Trail

Sylvia Gann Mahoney

The Great Western Trail (GWT), the last and longest of the major routes for driving Texas cattle to northern markets, has existed in the shadow of the famous Chisholm Trail, which ran approximately one hundred miles farther east. The trail had many names as it moved north two thousand miles.

Unobstructed grasslands provided passage for the Great Western for some nineteen years (1874–93) that cattle trailers used it. Those same grasslands, however, relegated the trail to obscurity, for the grass-dominated route lacked towns and cities with newspapers that might advertise and promote the route.

After the Civil War, young veterans returned to South Texas to find few jobs but millions of free-ranging longhorn cattle. At the same time, an Illinois entrepreneur, Joseph McCoy, assessed the growing eastern market for beef and the availability of longhorns and labor in South Texas. With railroads extending west, McCoy negotiated a railhead in Kansas. He sent circulars to South Texas promoting the merits of trailing cattle herds of 2,500 to 3,000 head to Kansas. Cattlemen and cowboys responded. In 1867 and afterward, such cattle-trailers, or drovers, moved herds north along the Chisholm Trail, also called the Eastern Trail, to McCoy's shipping site in Abilene, Kansas.

The federal Homestead Act of 1862, however, invited easterners to go west to claim 160 acres and begin farming. They did, especially in Kansas, and near the Chisholm Trail. Soon, trail-driven cattle trampled homesteaders'

The Great Western Cattle Trail. *Map by Sylvia Mahoney and David J. Murrah.*

farms, and domestic cattle died. The South Texas longhorns infected Kansas cattle with tick fever, something to which the longhorns were immune.

Kansas legislators, recognizing the economic boon that homesteaders created in their state, started closing parts of eastern Kansas to trail herds. After such closings, John T. Lytle, a South Texas cattleman and entrepreneur, beginning in 1874, turned his herds to the west. In Texas, he moved his route nearer to San Antonio and from there trailed them north through what is now Kerrville, Brady, Albany and Fort Griffin. Lytle crossed the Red River into Oklahoma at Doan's, a low-water crossing, pointed his animals north from there and delivered his first herd to Fort Robinson, Nebraska. The GWT had begun.

Drovers used many names for the Great Western Trail. They called each segment of it by the name of the next supply point. Thus, there were such names as the Fort Griffin–Doan's Crossing Trail. Farther north, it became the Dodge City Trail, the Ogallala Trail and in Canada the Texas Trail.

Drovers soon found that the unimpeded grasslands with rivers strategically located for watering herds extended northward across the Great Plains to Saskatchewan and Alberta in Canada. By 1879, after which Native Americans had been relegated to reservations and bison herds had been decimated, there was little to block drovers from moving cattle. The northern and eastern markets for South Texas cattle led to a thriving range-cattle industry stretching from the Mexican border into Canada.

Cattle trailed from Texas traded at railroad shipping points in Kansas and Nebraska, sold to federal agents on Indian reservations or, when marketed to ranchers, became the first herds on big-time ranges in Colorado, Wyoming, Nebraska, Montana and Canada.

The cattle industry boomed in the 1880s. But cattle-trailing slowed as railroads pushed on to the Great Plains and spread their lines into the Southwest. In the 1890s, long-distance cattle trailing ended.

Dedication of the first Great Western Trail (GWT) marker placed in Texas at Doan's Crossing north of Vernon. Pictured are, *left to right*, Texas Rotary GWT co-chairs Sylvia Mahoney and Jeff Bearden, Texas state representative Rick Hardcastle, Oklahoma state senator Bob Ker and Oklahoma GWT co-chairs Dennis Vernon and John Barton. *Courtesy Sylvia Mahoney.*

While subsequent histories, folklore, films and fiction kept the Chisholm Trail alive, at least in the public memory, the Great Western Trail was forgotten.

Then, in the 1930s, an Oklahoma man, P.P. Ackley, attempted to change the name of the GWT to Longhorn Chisholm Trail. He convinced the Texas Highway Department to place signs that marked the Chisholm. But he also placed the same signs on the GWT, promoting historical confusion and inaccuracies.

In 2003, a Chisholm Trail historian, Bob Klemme, challenged two Oklahomans to mark the Great Western Trail across their state. They, in turn, challenged Texans to do the same. The idea grew. By 2011, volunteers, many of whom were Rotarians, from Mexico, Canada and nine U.S. states (except Wyoming) had documented and marked the trail. As a result, the Great Western Trail has once again secured its place in history.

Chapter 13

Murdo Mackenzie and the Matador Ranch

Leland Turner

President Theodore Roosevelt once said, "During my term as president, [Murdo Mackenzie] was, on the whole, the most influential of the western cattle growers." Despite such high praise, Mackenzie's name is not one widely celebrated in western legend and lore. Successful but not colorful, Mackenzie was the antithesis of the stereotypical cattleman so prevalent in American popular culture. He was a successful corporate manager—a CEO—not a cowboy.

Murdo Mackenzie was born in County Ross, Scotland, in April 1850. He was an excellent student and entered the Royal Academy at Tain at the age of fourteen. Mackenzie apprenticed for a while in a local law office but soon took a position with a regional bank. Eventually, in January 1876, he became an assistant manager of the Balnagown Estate, where he mastered the intricacies of a large agricultural enterprise.

Given his training and experience, in 1885 Mackenzie secured a position with the Prairie Cattle Company, a Scottish capitalized operation based in Trinidad, Colorado. Mackenzie's effective financial management guided the Prairie Company through dire economic times and, in 1889, earned him a promotion to general manager.

His work at the Prairie Company caught the attention of another Scottish-financed ranching operation, the Matador Land and Cattle Company, headquartered in Motley County, Texas. Mackenzie became its general manager in January 1891. Over the next twenty years, he earned his place among the greatest cattlemen of the West.

Murdo Mackenzie was manager of the large Matador Land and Cattle Company for thirty-six years. *Courtesy Leland Turner.*

Mackenzie took over the Matador on the heels of an epic environmental disaster, the Big Die-Up, a series of droughts and blizzards between 1886 and 1888. The terrible weather ended the booming cattle industry, turning it from an adventure to a settled business.

In response, Mackenzie effectively introduced a new business plan to the big ranch. The plan involved a pasture management system, a breeding program and a water-use scheme using dams, irrigation ditches and windmills.

Over time, Mackenzie established Matador properties in Kansas, the Dakotas and Canada. In 1892, the Matador realized some $125,000 in gross sales and paid no dividends. Eight years later, the company was paying an annual 6.25 percent dividend, and in 1911, it added a 5 percent bonus. By then, annual sales exceeded a half million dollars. Mackenzie had successfully transformed a tenuous open-range cattle operation into a successful international ranching corporation.

More central to Mackenzie's national influence was his work with cattle raisers' organizations. When he was first involved with the Texas Cattle Raisers Association in 1893, the organization served a detective and protective role: battling cattle rustling and deterring the spread of diseases. Under Mackenzie's leadership, the Texas organization and a larger national group became politically active and, in particular, sought legislation to curtail the power of railroads.

After being elected president of the American National Live Stock Association in 1906, Mackenzie established a full-time office and lobbyist in Washington, D.C. With President Roosevelt a stalwart ally, the association influenced legislation that favored cattlemen. In particular, Mackenzie's livestock lobby wrote the first draft of the 1906 Hepburn Act, which struck at railroad's arbitrary ability to set freight rates and perhaps was the most important piece of railroad legislation to that time. When Mackenzie and his associates put the weight of their national organizations—the livestock lobby—behind an issue, the federal government listened, and its congressmen often took actions that favored western cattlemen.

Despite his growing influence in the United States, in January 1912 Mackenzie accepted a position in South America. He became manager of New York investor Percival Farquhar's Brazil Land and Cattle Company. Unfortunately, largely because of Farquhar's reckless speculations, the cattle empire became bankrupt by 1914. Mackenzie stayed on as manager until 1918, when, having fulfilled the terms of his contract, he returned to the United States.

Mackenzie joined the Matador Land and Cattle Company's board of directors and eventually returned as general manager of the ranch. He shepherded the operation through difficult times in the 1920s and 1930s.

When he died in 1937, Mackenzie had served the Matador for some thirty-six mostly successful years.

Clearly, Mackenzie was an influential cattleman. He effectively directed the Balnagown estate in Scotland, helped rescue the Colorado-based Prairie Cattle Company from bankruptcy, transformed the West Texas–based Matador ranch into a business operation paying handsome dividends to its Scottish investors and managed in Brazil what was at the time the largest cattle operation in the world.

Mackenzie introduced a thoughtful level of managed care and pasture supervision to large-scale cattle raising.

With each of the new and larger ranch operations he supervised, Murdo Mackenzie directed locally applicable innovations, but in the end, he essentially transferred Scottish agricultural knowledge to Brazil's frontier grasslands and to the great American western cattle industry.

Chapter 14

The IOA Ranch, Lubbock County, Texas

Don Abbe

The IOA Ranch, owned by the Western Land and Livestock Company, was established in 1884. The company chose the IOA brand because a number of its major investors were from the state of Iowa.

During 1884 and for several years afterward, the IOA ownership pieced together a continuous block of property stretching fourteen miles wide by thirty miles long. The main portion of the ranch contained roughly 420 sections (250,000 acres) of land. Additional piecemeal acquisitions in the northern half of the county brought the total ranch property—owned or leased—to about 330,000 acres.

The rectangular-shaped main portion of the IOA filled the southern half of Lubbock County. The original block consisted of both purchased and leased lands. And because it was not involved in later court proceedings, the far western half of the large spread probably represented a significant portion of the parcels leased from neighboring landowners.

The IOA headquarters was located in the southeastern part of the county on the first three sections of land the company purchased from Zach Williams in 1885.

From its beginning, the IOA struggled. Thus, in 1887, the Western Land and Livestock Company sent Frank Wheelock, a great-nephew of one of the ranch's principal stockholders, Stillman Wheelock, to monitor and manage the floundering cattle operation. Despite Wheelock's best efforts, the ranch proved unsuccessful. Plummeting beef prices, a drought in the mid-1880s and viciously cold and bitter winters during those same years

Before it became the Boles Ranch, this compound in Ransom Canyon east of Lubbock served as the IOA Ranch headquarters. *Courtesy Southwest Collection, Texas Tech University.*

led to a collapse of large ranches all across the West. The IOA was one of hundreds that failed during the late 1880s and early 1890s.

When it was apparent the ranch was not going to succeed, corporation leaders determined to jettison the land and cattle in as orderly a way as possible. They directed Wheelock to sell the cattle during a three-year period between 1893 and 1896. Once the cattle were removed, the owners turned the borrowed lands back to the state or to persons from whom sections had been rented—mainly by letting the leases lapse. After 1896, they planned to sell sections the company owned outright.

By the time of the decision to liquidate the ranch, Frank Wheelock had become a leader in the local community. Indeed, he was a principal founder of Lubbock.

Three years ahead of schedule, Wheelock began to sell some of the most desirable lands to his friends and area ranchers. As a result of the early land sales, a Western Land and Livestock Company stockholder, Quincy A. Shaw, sued to block sales and foreclose on those lands already sold. Shaw, a wealthy Boston investor who may have held a majority of the company stock, was unhappy about the sales. Shaw complained when Wheelock began to sell off the choice lands, with proceeds going to the company and not to Shaw as the first lien holder. In 1894, he filed a legal suit against Wheelock, the Western Land and Livestock Company and all persons who had purchased lands from the company.

The suit wound its way through the local courts and on to an appeals court. In March 1901, the court decided for Quincy Shaw. Land still owned by the IOA and land sold by Wheelock were ordered foreclosed, and the court ordered a sheriff's sale be held to dispose of all lands owned by the ranch. The sale occurred on November 1, 1901. The Kokernot Ranch family, with holdings in far west Texas, bought the entire ranch, which at that time consisted of just over 100,000 acres. Most of the Kokernot-purchased land was in the southeastern part of Lubbock County. It contained about one-fifth of the county's land.

The Kokernots with their O6 brand had no intention of staying in the Lubbock area. L.M. and Herbert Lee Kokernot viewed the purchase of the IOA as a simple but effective way to enhance their other ranching operations and make money. Farmers, the Kokernots reasoned, were moving onto the Llano Estacado in the late 1890s and afterward, and they saw a chance to buy IOA range land at a low price and then sell it for more to farmer-settlers.

Within a decade, the best of the former IOA ranch property had gone to farmers. By 1915, several small ranches had emerged from the sale of lands not suited to farming. By then, the IOA was little more than a footnote in the history of Lubbock.

Chapter 15

The Llano Estacado, Mexico and Gulf Railroad

Paul H. Carlson

At the turn of the century in 1900 and afterward, nearly every town booster understood the importance of railroads. Railroads could make or unmake a community. They could lower transportation costs and shorten travel time for both people and commodities. Leaders in every town wanted one.

The Llano Estacado, Mexico and Gulf (LEM&G) represented such a railroad. Although never built, it was promoted with gusto, especially in Shafter Lake, a short-lived community founded in 1907 in Andrews County.

The railroad was to run from Dalhart in the Texas Panhandle south through the heart of the Llano Estacado to Mexico and the Gulf Coast. Promoters said it would connect with the Texas and Pacific, the Southern Pacific, the Fort Worth and Denver and other lines.

According to James T. Cumley, editor and publisher of the Shafter Lake newspaper, the LEM&G would place his "city of the plains" within a night's ride of Fort Worth and Dallas. It would "give us direct connection," Cumley wrote, via the Southern Pacific with both the Atlantic and Pacific coasts. He envisioned the railroad eventually running as far south as Chihuahua City, Mexico.

Cumley's promotion was fantastic. In 1907, he predicted in his newspaper, the *Shafter Lake Herald*, that within two years Shafter Lake would have a population of five thousand inhabitants, that the railroad would be completed and that his Andrews County community would serve as a major terminal for the line. The railroad, Cumley said, would make Shafter Lake the largest cattle shipping point in Texas outside of Fort Worth and brand his community as "the most rapidly growing city in the GOLDEN west."

Others shared Cumley's enthusiasm. Will N. Waddell of Odessa, one of several West Texas bankers interested in the railroad, surveyed the country south toward the Rio Grande and the connecting tracks of the Southern Pacific.

J.A. Card, a contract surveyor, in August 1907 visited Shafter Lake with a small crew. He conducted a preliminary survey of the town, according to Cumley's newspaper, to determine the location of a railway yard, a roundhouse and a depot. Card indicated that the railroad would approach the city from the southwest and reach the lake directly south of town. The yard and roundhouse would be located on the east side of the lake, a small body of water lying well below the elevation of the surrounding country. The lake would be converted into a reservoir to supply water for both the railroad and the city. Card believed the reservoir would hold about eight million gallons of water, or enough, he said, to supply a city of twenty-five thousand citizens.

In September 1907, a Fort Worth newspaper, the *Record*, carried information on the proposed line's construction capital. Indicating that the project was almost fully financed, the paper claimed that the Santa Fe Railroad was a principal backer and that resources also included money from Chicago, Kansas City and West Texas.

Despite the financial backing and the surveying activity, the railroad proved to be a phantom, little more than the fabulous dream of a fervent town promoter.

A few miles of track may have been laid south of Dalhart, but the line was abandoned and eventually torn up. Dalhart sources knew little of the LEM&G and reasoned that the new construction in its area represented branch lines for the Rock Island Railroad or the Fort Worth and Denver.

Mystery enshrouds the entire enterprise. The names of the West Texas bankers, except for Waddell, were never revealed. Cumley, who first broke news of the railroad capitalists, was, for business reasons, he wrote, asked not to divulge their names. Rather, he said, they were qualified railway men and confidently predicted that when it was apprised of their identity, the public would have no doubt that the six men were of the highest integrity with unquestionable financial standing.

Cumley circulated a map of the rail line's proposed route, but he made no mention of where it would hook up with the Southern Pacific or where it would cross the Rio Grande. In August 1907, the *Shafter Lake Herald* noted

The Llano Estacado, Mexico and Gulf Railroad was the unfulfilled dream of town promoter James Cumley and others. *Courtesy Diane McLaurin.*

that its trackage would exceed six hundred miles. Two months later, the line's total length was set at four hundred miles.

In the end, neither Shafter Lake nor the LEM&G succeeded. In 1910, the town reached the peak of its growth with a population of about five hundred inhabitants. It boasted of a bank, church, schoolhouse, general store, blacksmith shop and small but modern hotel. After losing a close election to Andrews for location of the county seat, Shafter Lake declined rapidly.

The railroad—the Llano Estacado, Mexico and Gulf—was a six-month pipe dream, proving to be little more than an excited and overzealous town promoter's fantasy.

Chapter 16

Ozark Trails Roadways in West Texas

Paul H. Carlson

The Ozark Trails movement was a publicity scheme, but it was also an effort in the early twentieth century to promote good highways. The trails existed through much of Arkansas and its bordering states, including Texas, and at first, they were aimed at getting people to the Ozark Mountain vacation resort of William Hope "Coin" Harvey, a lawyer, presidential campaign organizer, political tract writer, promoter and hotel builder.

More importantly, the Ozark Trails promoted better highways and greater automobile travels, and they did much—though the amount might be hard to measure—in West Texas. They represented a forerunner to Route 66, helped to create the Texas Highway Department, encouraged such roads as the Bankhead Highway through Texas and otherwise promoted the use of automobiles for overland travel.

In 1900, William Harvey purchased 320 acres of land near Rogers, Arkansas. The next year, he began developing the site as a major—and fabulous—health and vacation retreat. He built a five-mile-long railroad from the town of Lowell in the state's extreme northwest corner to a depot near his resort, which he called Monte Ne, or "mountain waters." Harvey had big plans for his sophisticated health spa, but they did not all work out. In 1910, he abandoned the railroad between Lowell and Monte Ne.

With the railroad's demise, Harvey needed an alternate access to his resort. Thus was born in 1913 the Ozark Trails Association (OTA), designed to promote a series of improved roadways connecting his isolated health spa to four adjacent states.

Harvey and his Ozark Trails Association did not plan to build the roads. Rather, they wanted to promote good roads and educate local communities on various economic advantages for improved highways. They also provided information on highway design. Local folks, they hoped, would build and maintain the roads, and the association would promote and publicize and, by extension, get people to Monte Ne.

Interest grew. By 1916, Oklahoma City had replaced Monte Ne as the headquarters for the Ozark Trails Association, and that year, seven thousand OTA delegates attended a convention in the city. The next year, reportedly, between ten and twenty thousand people attended an OTA meeting in Amarillo, thus temporarily doubling the city's population.

For West Texas, an important result of the meeting was the establishment of several Ozark Trails' highways or branch routes. Many towns wanted to be part of the system—at least they did if they were not part of some other major named highway, such as the Bankhead. To be designated as part of the trail, some towns agreed to pay the OTA and to put up signs or posters to mark the route.

There was as yet no national or Texas system of numbered highways. Named highways, such as the Lincoln and Bankhead, were increasing in number, and promoters sought markers, signs and other insignia to identify their roads. They might put colored ribbons on trees in rural areas or paint their symbol on barns, boulders or telephone poles. Some highways built concrete posts.

Ozark Trail marker at Dimmitt, Texas. *Courtesy Dan K. Utley.*

The Ozark Trails highways used diamond-shaped signs with a white background and a green "OT" between two green stripes.

After 1918, the OTA encouraged towns to build pyramids or obelisks. The plan called for approximately twenty-five-foot-tall concrete pyramids, painted white and green, with a bit of travel information and with lights for illumination that helped travelers at night. The number of obelisks built is unknown, but they appeared in Missouri, Arkansas, Oklahoma, New Mexico and Texas. Only seven of them survive.

In West Texas, the obelisks appeared in Wellington, Estelline, Memphis, Farwell, Tulia, Dimmit, Nazareth, Tampico Station (in Hall County) and perhaps elsewhere along an old southern route of the Ozark Trails. The Texas pyramids survive in four places: Tulia, Dimmitt, Wellington and Tampico Station (now an abandoned crossroads). Two markers survive in Oklahoma and one in New Mexico.

In the 1920s, the Ozark Trails highway system reached its peak. A numbering system on both national and state levels to identify highways had begun, and as it expanded, the need for named highways declined.

The old northern route of the Ozark Trails across Oklahoma and through the Texas Panhandle became Route 66. The OT's southern route declined in favor of various numbered highways.

Except for the few concrete obelisks that remain, Ozark Trails highways exist today only in memory. Yet Ozark Trails and the OTA aided travelers, promoted better roads and highways, supported the creation of highway departments and encouraged construction and maintenance of good roadways. They were at once both the result of an older "Good Roads" movement and the precursor of modern numbered highways.

Part III
Town Builders

The early history of Lubbock can be characterized by interesting, dynamic leaders, both men and women. Men dominated the establishment of the little town on the plains, but women, such as Mollie Abernathy and Mae Simmons, came to play important roles in its development or in its remarkable education of minority students.

If hotel registration records are correct, the town was informally founded in late 1889 on land just east of what became the Lubbock Country Club. A year later, spurred by a nearby and competing community, Lubbock leaders, including Frank Wheelock, in late 1890 joined forces with their rivals, led by Whit Rayner, to establish modern Lubbock.

George Singer, Isham Tubbs and even the magnificent—for its day—two-story Nicolett Hotel also played key roles in the founding of Lubbock, and except for the inanimate hotel, they—together with the others—must be considered Lubbock town builders.

Chapter 17

George Singer and His Yellow House Store

Henry B. Crawford

George W. Singer operated a store in Yellow House Draw a decade before Lubbock became a town. Born in Ohio in 1844, he married Rachael Underhill in 1878. The Underhills were followers of Quaker leader Elijah Paris Cox, who in 1879 founded in northeastern Lubbock County the settlement that became Estacado.

After a brief period with the Quakers in Estacado, Singer established a store at what is now known as the Lubbock Lake Landmark State Historic Site along Yellow House Draw, in northwest present-day Lubbock. Two military roads crossed there: one from Fort Elliot south to Fort Stockton, the other from Fort Griffin westward to Fort Sumner, New Mexico. Both roads followed long-established trade routes, perfect for a place of commerce.

When they settled at the lake about 1881, the Singers lived in their wagon and a tent while George worked on building a dugout. Singer's closest neighbors were at the Zach Williams' sheep ranch, some miles southeast down the canyon near the Buffalo Springs. Today, the Williams property is occupied by the V-8 Ranch.

After a railroad arrived at Colorado City in 1881, Singer hauled lumber and merchandise from the town to build and equip his store. The building was about eighteen by twenty feet with no windows, but it had front and back doors. Singer also built a house with two fourteen- by fourteen-foot rooms a short distance from the store.

Rachael Singer, who enjoyed a reputation as a fine cook, operated an "eating place" in the back of the store. It was the first public restaurant in

George Singer and family, circa 1891. *Courtesy Southwest Collection, Texas Tech University.*

Lubbock County. She was known everywhere for her biscuits, and travelers from a wide area stopped to try them.

Singer's store was a popular establishment. Cattle drovers routed their drives so they could stop at Singer's for food and hospitality. Often, visitors dropped in for a bit of late-evening poker and comradeship. If some of them needed an additional poker stake, candy or tobacco from the store's shelves would do. Players were trusted to pay Singer back, and they always did. Open credit was the rule at Singer's. After store hours, customers simply took what goods they needed and left a list with a promise to pay later. Some stayed all night, which probably qualifies the store as the first "hotel" in the area.

Indian passersby were also fond of the hard candy that the Singers kept on hand. Rachael Singer often treated them to biscuits.

Not all visitors were friendly. In 1886, a stranger arrived at the store. After feeding him a meal and giving him a paper sack of cookies, Rachael allowed him to stay overnight in the store. Sometime later, George Singer went to check on the visitor and was met with a hail of gunfire. Singer ran to the house to get his rifle, and during a subsequent gunfire exchange, smoke began coming from the store. Before anyone could react, the store exploded, probably from the supply of ammunition and kegs of powder stocked within. Nothing was left but a pile of ashes. The remains of the intruder were found and buried.

Sometime later, a hunting party of Comanches amused themselves by tramping their horses through the store's ashes. On their return, they presented the Singers with a freshly butchered buffalo calf.

After the fire, Singer determined to protect the house. Accordingly, Rachael drove a wagon to Colorado City and there bought lumber and fresh supplies. She made the 250-mile round trip alone and without incident. The Singers built a new store and before long were back in business.

Singer's store stocked many useful goods, including crackers and canned meats. The Singers also carried guns of all kinds, paint, lard, blankets, saddles, tack, rope, flour and cornmeal. Customers remembered seeing canned sardines and salmon, cheese, sacks of grain or potatoes and barrels of flour piled among boxes containing Arbuckle's coffee, lard, beans and other canned goods. The store also stocked boots, bridles, blankets, ammunition and overalls. Bull Durham tobacco was prominent.

For a time in the 1880s, Singer's Yellow House store served as an area post office. During winter months, it was a warm refuge in an otherwise empty environment. Singer never locked it.

In 1891, the Singers relocated the business to the new and nearby fledgling town of Lubbock. They remained there for about seven years before moving to Kansas, where George Singer died in 1910.

Frontier mercantile establishments like Singer's store were good places to congregate and exchange news. Singer's customers ranged from cattlemen to Indians, from hunters to soldiers and businessmen.

In some ways, Singer's store was the birthplace of Lubbock.

Chapter 18

W.E. Rayner, a Founder of Lubbock

Paul H. Carlson

Whitfield Elijah "Whit" Rayner (1854–1907) was a principal founder of Lubbock, a rancher and a real estate entrepreneur. He operated ranches in Stonewall, King and Knox Counties and was partial owner of Rayner Cattle Company. He played a key role in the establishment of Lubbock in 1890 and, late in life, ran a land agency in Stamford, Texas.

Born in Memphis, Tennessee, Rayner was well educated. Tall, perhaps six feet, four inches, with black hair and black eyes, he was striking in appearance but hot tempered and quick to anger. He did not serve in the military, but his ranch cowboys called him "Captain."

Rayner moved to Saint Louis about 1878 and opened a wholesale business. A year later, he established the Rayner Cattle Company and shifted his operation to Texas. He built his first headquarters at Mockingbird Springs on the Brazos River in Knox County.

In the late 1880s, Rayner acquired a ranch in Stonewall County—the Call Bar, he named it. He also established the town of Rayner near the county's eastern edge and on his ranch, and he helped organize the county.

He helped to build a small, wood-frame courthouse in Rayner, encouraged others to settle in the village and in 1889 got the town named the seat of Stonewall County. Two or three years later, town and county leaders, including Whit Rayner, built a magnificent rock and stone structure to replace the original courthouse. The town of Rayner, with about 250 to 300 people, remained the county seat for ten years, after which in June 1898 it lost to Aspermont in a bitter vote over changing the county seat location.

The old Rayner courthouse in Stonewall County near Aspermont, 2002. *Courtesy Paul Carlson.*

The village of Rayner soon disappeared, but its large stone courthouse remained. Sometime after the removal of county records to Aspermont, authorities sold the building to Miss Johnnie Colbert, a popular local teacher. Colbert hoped to start a college at the building but was unsuccessful, and the county soon repossessed the old courthouse.

County commissioners in 1915 sold the structure to J.R. Baldwin. In 1936, the Texas Historical Commission, as part of the state's Centennial Celebration, placed a marker in its yard. Then, in 1945, Baldwin's son, M.A. "Fuzz" Baldwin, and his wife moved into the house and modernized it. The former courthouse became a majestic home, and local lore suggests it was a model for the huge ranch home in the popular 1956 Hollywood film *Giant*. Today, the building is abandoned, falling into disrepair and sits forlorn on high ground less than one-half mile off U.S. Highway 380 near Old Glory.

In the meantime, Whit Rayner became involved in the founding of Lubbock. He joined with W.D. Crump, H.M. Bandy and D.F. Goss to establish a town. They quickly split, however, as Rayner wanted to place the town at a different location. Crump, Bandy and Goss joined with Frank Wheelock and Rollie Burns, who had a village of several businesses, about fifty people and a large eighteen-room hotel—the Nicolett Hotel—operating north of the canyon and east of the present Lubbock Country Club. They called their village Lubbock.

Rayner and his nephew, Howard Rayner, purchased a town site just north of present Jones AT&T Stadium. They marked out a town, sold lots and persuaded several people, including George Wolffarth and Will and Van Sanders, to join them. Their village, which residents called South Lubbock, soon boasted of thirty-seven buildings and about fifty residents, including George Singer, one of the first businessmen in the area. Lubbock and South Lubbock stood less than four miles apart.

The Rayner and Wheelock-Burns contingents each sought recognition of their community as the county seat. Both groups realized that in losing a county seat vote, their little town would decline and probably disappear. Accordingly, in the fall of 1890, the village rivals met on several occasions to resolve the predicament. On December 17, led by Frank Wheelock of Lubbock and Whit Rayner, whose community was now called Monterey, they signed an agreement to combine their nascent towns at a third location, present downtown Lubbock. They further agreed to move all homes and businesses, including the large Nicolett Hotel, to the new town site.

With the Lubbock issues settled, Rayner went back to his namesake community and his ranch. Then, after losing out to Aspermont in the county seat struggle there, he sold his Stonewall County property and moved to Stamford to engage in real estate enterprises. He died in 1907, after having been gored by a bull.

Chapter 19

Frank Wheelock

Jennifer Spurrier

Like other entities, the village of Lubbock had several founding fathers. Frank Emerson Wheelock (1863–1932) was one of them. Wheelock played a prominent role in establishing the town and for many years afterward was instrumental in developing the city.

Frank E. Wheelock was born in Erie County, New York, on April 11, 1863. His father, Dr. William Efner Wheelock, was a physician. His mother was Louisa Diane Farrington Wheelock, but she died while Frank was a child. Frank had one brother, William.

After the passing of his wife, Dr. Wheelock moved to Madison, Wisconsin. Later, he purchased land in and moved to North Dakota. Although they spent each summer with their father, the boys went to live with uncles to attend school the rest of the year. William went to the home of his uncle and aunt in Moline, Illinois. Frank lived with his uncle Dr. Jerome B. Wheelock in Madison for a time, but the physician relocated often. He moved his family, including Frank, to Moline, Illinois, and in 1878, they resided in Minneapolis, Minnesota.

Frank Wheelock finished his secondary education in Minneapolis. His first job upon graduation was with a local fruit commission merchant, S.J. Palmer. Subsequently, he worked in a number of enterprises.

In 1887, Frank moved to Texas. He became a manager of the IOA Ranch in Lubbock County. The ranch, established in 1884, consisted of 136 sections (86,940 acres) spread across the southern half of the as-yet-unorganized county. The northern boundary of the large ranch ran east and west along approximately present Nineteenth Street.

Frank and Sylvia Belle Hunt Wheelock, circa 1892. *Courtesy Southwest Collection, Texas Tech University.*

The Western Land and Livestock Company owned the IOA, and Wheelock's great-uncle Stillman Wheelock of Moline was a major director of the company.

Financially, the ranch did not prosper. Drought, harsh weather, volatile cattle prices, theft and other issues prevented the ranch from making a profit. Stillman Wheelock died in1892, and a year later, ranch owners began selling portions of the large property. Frank continued as manager of the IOA until it shut down in 1901.

In the meantime, Frank Wheelock engaged in additional enterprises. With others in 1888 and 1889, the twenty-five-year-old ranch manager built the large Nicolett Hotel, which he named, and established a little village on high ground just east of the modern Lubbock Country Club. In early 1891, after a complicated agreement with rival town builders, Wheelock and his partners moved the hotel and the entire village four miles south to Lubbock's present downtown square.

Wheelock also operated his own ranch, the Locust Grove Ranch, of seven sections (4,480 acres), in the Lubbock area. He bred registered cattle and raised horses. In addition, he became part owner of a store with Irvin L. Hunt.

As Lubbock and the county grew, Wheelock played an active role in both communities. He served on the first county commission. He became the first postmaster for the city. He won an election as the first mayor of the town of Lubbock and served two terms.

Clippings from a Wheelock family scrapbook show that for several years, he was Democratic Party chairman for Lubbock County. According to Seymour Connor, he "donated the first plot for the Lubbock cemetery," and he aided in building the first cotton gin in the county.

After Lubbock County was organized in 1891, Frank Wheelock became the first man to marry in the county. He wed Sylva Belle Hunt on December 9, 1891. The Wheelocks had seven children: Cyril Efner, Eva Minnette (Mrs. John Jarrott), Elwin Bryan, Howard Emerson, Fern Marie (Mrs. E.M. Conley), William Irvin and Edith Annette (Mrs. T.T. Tipps).

In 1906, a scholar wrote, "Frank E. Wheelock has been a foremost man of affairs and influence in Lubbock County from before its time of organization." And, "Mr. Wheelock, being a man of great business energy and force of character, has naturally been foremost in various enterprises and events which have taken place in the history of the county."

Clearly, as early as 1906, Wheelock had already done much for the county. He continued to serve for many years, remaining an active citizen until his passing on June 28, 1932. He was sixty-nine.

On the morning of his death, Wheelock had been out at the city cemetery hoeing weeds. At the time, he was president of the cemetery association. Frank Emerson Wheelock served his communities—Lubbock and Lubbock County—in leadership roles until his last day.

Chapter 20

The Founding of Lubbock

Paul H. Carlson

About twelve to fourteen people, led by Frank E. Wheelock and Whit E. Rayner, established modern Lubbock in mid-December 1890. For several months prior, several men involved in the town's beginning met on an irregular basis at the Nicolett Hotel, located in the village of Lubbock (often misnamed in historical literature as North Town or North Lubbock) just east of present-day Lubbock Country Club. The men sought to iron out difficulties and differences in founding a town that would be the judicial and administrative seat of Lubbock County.

The story is complicated. Three separate groups wanted to establish such a county seat town. Wheelock, Rollie Burns and other investors, including some from Dallas, had built the Nicolett Hotel and had established their village of Lubbock. In December 1890, the community contained fifty people and about thirty-seven structures, including the large and imposing hotel.

A second group, led by W.D. Crump, H.M. Bandy and D.F. Goss, also included Whit Rayner of Stonewall County but only briefly. These promoters secured land near the modern Lubbock Country Club, but they did not get a village laid out, and Rayner split from the others over a disagreement about location. After he left, the others joined the Wheelock-Burns coalition, and in essence, the second group disbanded.

Rayner, his nephew Howard Rayner and a few others composed the third group. In August, they established a tiny burgh just north of present-day Jones AT&T Stadium. It grew quickly and in December contained

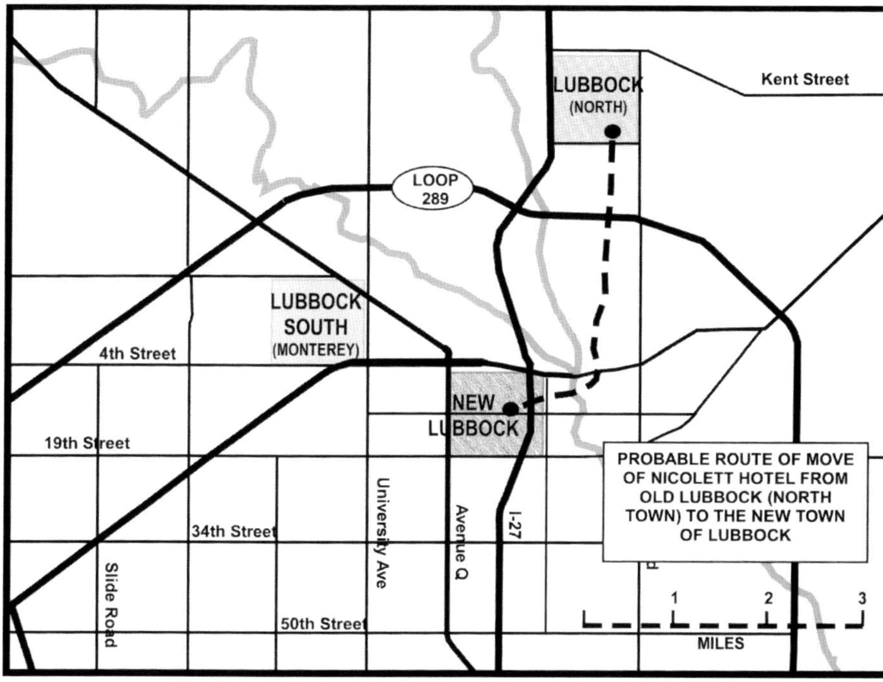

Sites of the original Lubbock town site, Rayner's town of Monterey, the new Lubbock town site and the approximate route used to move the Nicolett Hotel. *Map by David J. Murrah.*

thirty-two structures and about fifty residents. People living there referred to their community by various names, including Lubbock South and South Lubbock. During the last week of its existence, the town became known as Monterey.

For Lubbock and Monterey, a serious problem existed. The communities were located not quite four miles apart. If one of them was named the county seat, the other, because of the proximity, would likely decline and become a ghost town.

Such an event had occurred in other counties, including Rayner's own Stonewall County. His town of Rayner had served for ten years as the county seat but subsequently lost a county seat election to Aspermont. Not long afterward, the town of Rayner died. On the old Rayner town site, only a large, decaying building, the former county courthouse, remains. It stands south of present U.S. Highway 380 on the east side of the county.

So, to avoid a county seat fight, men representing the interests of Lubbock and Lubbock South met often over lunch or dinner at the Nicolett Hotel.

Paul Carlson with the bell that hung in the Nicolett Hotel. *Courtesy Monte Monroe.*

Their discussions continued through September, October, November and the first half of December 1890.

The leaders worked through several issues. They selected a new location and purchased a section of land centered at the present downtown courthouse square. They decided the name of the new town would be the same as the county, "Lubbock," which was named for Thomas S. Lubbock, a Civil War veteran whose brother Francis had been governor of Texas between 1861 and 1863. They determined how town lots should be divided among all those involved in the town founding.

They finished their "merger" discussions on December 17, 1890. Two days later, fourteen men—eight (Frank Wheelock, Rollie Burns, H.M. Bandy, W.D. Crump, George M. Hunt, John T. Lofton, James Harrison and Henry C. Hiatt) representing Lubbock and six (Whit Rayner, Howard Rayner, Van Sanders, W.A. Carlisle, George C. Wolffarth and Joseph Lang) from the now-named Monterey community—signed a lengthy agreement spelling out terms of the merger.

Wheelock and Rayner took the signed document to Estacado, still the county seat of Crosby County. Because Lubbock County remained under political and administrative jurisdiction of its neighboring entity, Wheelock and Rayner recorded the document with the county clerk there.

Thus, Lubbock was formally established. Physical establishment came quickly afterward. Within thirty days, most buildings from the rival factions had been moved to lots near the present downtown square. By the end of February 1891, even the large and elegant Nicolett Hotel had been relocated to a spot across the street from the square. Frank Wheelock and Rollie Burns oversaw its move southward and then down a gentle slope in what today is Mackenzie Park, across Yellow House Draw, up a gentle slope out of the draw and from there to the new Lubbock location.

When leaders organized Lubbock County in 1891, Lubbock became its county seat. By that time, the new community was the voters' only choice.

Chapter 21

The Nicolett Hotel

Paul H. Carlson

As evidenced by the previous sections of this part, the Nicolett Hotel figures prominently in the early history of Lubbock. According to its first register, owners Frank E. Wheelock and Rollie Burns built it in late 1888 and early 1889.

The owners constructed the prominent hotel on high prairie land just east of the present Lubbock Country Club, where the business park is located. The original village of Lubbock, with thirty-seven buildings and a population of fifty people, stood there. Wheelock, manager of the IOA Ranch that once covered much of Lubbock County, named it the Nicolett Hotel, entitling it after the Nicolet Hotel in Minneapolis, a city in which he briefly lived.

When finished in 1889, the hotel was an imposing structure. A two-and-one-half-story, eighteen-room, white-painted building, with a half-story attic lighted and ventilated by dormer windows, it could be seen from miles away. The big, square, wood-frame hotel contained a porch across its entire front and a large second-story balcony over the wide porch. Its interior was, at least for pioneer Texas in 1889, plush and elegant, with a couple of lounge chairs in the lobby and a traditional but elaborate front desk.

One historian argued it was "the largest hotel in West Texas at the time." George W. Hunt, according to Seymour Connor, moved from Estacado to Lubbock to manage the hotel.

For constructing the Nicolett Hotel, Wheelock, Burns and their partners got lumber, supplies and furnishings at Amarillo, which provided the most practical access to a railroad in 1888. Freighting the material overland to

The Nicolett Hotel as it originally stood on the high ground at the present business park in northeast Lubbock, about five miles north of present-day downtown. After its move to the new town of Lubbock, the cover over the second-story balcony was not replaced. *Courtesy Southwest Collection, Texas Tech University.*

Lubbock was not cheap. The trip took four days and cost one dollar per ton for the material.

The finished hotel contained a popular restaurant. The expense of meals at the restaurant was probably standard for 1889 and 1890 but inexpensive in terms of 2016 prices. On May 19, 1889, for example, Green C. Igo, one of the pioneers of Lubbock County, paid a total of one dollar for meals for three people.

And the iconic beef steak of western cowboy days was not the only fare on the menu. According to the hotel register, on June 14, 1889, twenty-seven individuals, apparently single young people from Estacado, enjoyed an oyster dinner at the hotel.

Consider this comparison: the fancy Nicolett Hotel stood prominently in a village of only fifty people. About fifteen miles away, in the ten-year-old town of Estacado with two hundred people, two general stores, a

Rollie Burns, pictured here with his wife, Mary, and family in 1888, was one of the owners of the Nicolett Hotel. *Courtesy Southwest Collection, Texas Tech University.*

lawyer's office, a newspaper office, the Crosby County Courthouse and a meetinghouse that doubled as church and school, stood another hotel. But the Estacado hotel's restaurant, which was detached from the main building, contained a dirt floor, uncovered plank walls through which wind blew and a canvas roof.

The large, stylish Nicolett Hotel attracted many visitors, some for a meal while they were in the village and, of course, overnight travelers, including salesmen (drummers), cowboys, real estate agents and land and town promoters.

Among the more determined and successful promoters who stopped at the hotel was Whit E. Rayner of Stonewall County. Rayner and his supporters, including his nephew Howard Rayner, in the summer of 1890 laid out and platted a town just north of present Jones AT&T Stadium on the Texas Tech University campus. Rayner's town, called South Lubbock at the time, soon held about thirty-two buildings and a population of fifty people.

The hamlets of Lubbock and South Lubbock were only about four miles apart. Leaders in both tiny communities wanted their town to become the county seat. But promoters in both places knew that after an election for county seat, the losing village would disappear. Accordingly, through the summer and fall of 1890, the rival leaders met often at the Nicolett Hotel to hammer out a compromise.

On December 17, with Rayner's town now called Monterey, they reached an agreement and two days later signed a document that, among other things, consolidated the two towns at the present city's downtown square and named the new community Lubbock. They further agreed that within thirty days, all buildings and people from Monterey and the original Lubbock should move to the new town, but the hotel might take longer.

It did, of course, but in February 1891, Frank Wheelock, Rollie Burns and their supporters moved the Nicolett Hotel, minus its front porch and balcony, about five miles south and a bit west to the square in the new Lubbock town. Here, the hotel's managers used a large bell to call lunch and dinner guests to its tables. Here also, through change in ownership and management and through remodeling and additions, but always absent the old second-story balcony cover, the Nicolett Hotel served the city's citizens and visitors for many years.

Chapter 22

Mollie Abernathy

June Steele

Mollie Abernathy (1866–1960), from a prominent ranching family in Hood County, moved to the South Plains with her husband, James Jarrott, in 1902. The couple had filed on a one-mile-wide strip of land about thirty miles southwest of Lubbock and running to the New Mexico state line. They brought their four children and twenty-three other families with them to settle the vacant property.

The area was ranching country characterized by large operations, such as the Lake-Tomb Cattle Company, whose owners leased their grazing land from the state or from railroad companies. Cattlemen became upset as the farmer-settlers began to buy and live on the land.

James Jarrott, whom cattlemen held accountable for bringing in the new residents, began receiving both written and oral threats on his life. Mollie said the hostile ranchers believed that getting rid of Jarrott would scare settlers away.

On August 28, 1902, sixteen days after he stood in front of the Lubbock courthouse to secure title to the property, Jarrott was gunned down at a Lake-Tomb windmill, located three miles south of present-day Ropesville southwest of Lubbock.

At a judicial hearing concerning her husband's death, Mollie testified about what she knew regarding her husband's murder, but the hearing concluded without resolution. Lubbock County did not have money or manpower to investigate the shooting fully.

The murder remained a mystery until 1933, when a gunman named "Deacon" Jim Miller, about to be hanged for numerous offenses, confessed

Mollie Abernathy was a Lubbock businesswoman and philanthropist who provided land for present-day Mackenzie Park in Lubbock. *Courtesy Southwest Collection, Texas Tech University.*

in Ada, Oklahoma, to having shot the unarmed Jarrott some thirty years earlier.

Mollie became determined that her husband's death not be in vain. Getting on with the business of starting her cattle ranch, she hired a few hands, built a herd of one thousand cattle, added to her landholdings and constructed a large two-story house—all on the property some thirty miles southwest of Lubbock.

As the area grew in population, Mollie's ranch came to occupy a crossroads. Years later, she said, the "house…was like a hotel—two main roads went by it. I got acquainted with these railroad people. They'd pass by and stop at the house and then end up staying the night."

In the meantime, not long after Jarrott's death, Mollie became acquainted with Monroe Abernathy, a businessman from Lubbock. Mollie owned several lots in the town, and Monroe, like Mollie, worked in the land business. They became close friends and in 1904 were engaged. Monroe asked her about an engagement ring, but true to form, Mollie said she preferred instead a particular piece of property that Monroe owned be deeded over to her. The town lots, situated near Avenue J and Broadway in Lubbock, became among the most valuable in the city.

A short time later, the Santa Fe Railroad began considering a rail line to Lubbock. Monroe Abernathy's knowledge of the land and his acquaintance with railroad officials made him an effective liaison between Lubbock and the railroad. Monroe, with others, convinced officials to build tracks south from Amarillo through Plainview to Lubbock. They agreed, and on October 25, 1909, Lubbock got its first railroad.

Towns began to spring up along the route, and railroad officials invited Mollie to name two of the communities. She chose "Abernathy" for one. The other she named "Monroe," but after four small school districts consolidated in the 1930s, the town's name was changed to "New Deal."

In 1919, the Abernathys, who had been centralizing their business and social activities in Lubbock, moved to town. They sold the ranch and cattle business a year later, settled on the one thousand acres they owned on the east and northeast edge of Lubbock and turned their attention to urban civic life.

The Abernathy holdings in Lubbock included some of the most beautiful terrain on the South Plains: part of Yellow House Canyon where two water courses, Blackwater and Yellow House Draws, merge to form the North Fork of the Double Mountain Fork of the Brazos River.

In 1924, the Abernathys donated 138 acres of the canyon property close to their primary residence, near Quirt Avenue (present MLK) and Park Boulevard, to the city for "City Park Number 1"—part of present Mackenzie Park.

Mollie Abernathy lived a fruitful life. She was a rancher who became an urban businesswoman. She bought, expanded and remodeled the Nicolett Hotel before selling it to finance other construction. She was a philanthropist who remained active in Lubbock political and civic affairs.

Chapter 23

Isham Tubbs

Jack Becker

In many ways, Isham Tubbs (1852–1947) typified early pioneers who settled Lubbock County. A native of East Texas who moved his family to Lubbock in 1890, he planned to ranch on land opening up in West Texas at the turn of the last century.

He moved west, like many other Americans, with a network of extended family members, including his two brothers-in-law and their families. Isham and the entire Tubbs clan played important roles in the development of Lubbock, especially its religious, educational and civil organizations. They put down roots, raised their families and undertook a number of enterprises that benefited themselves and their community.

Most early pioneers who moved to Lubbock County, including the Tubbs family, lived in dugout homes. In all likelihood, the home Tubbs and his son Oscar built was a half-dugout, as the layer of caliche rocks (the caprock) found just below the surface prevented them from digging more than a few feet into the ground. Their first home was probably twelve by sixteen feet and built out of materials that could be obtained locally: rocks, tree branches, old buffalo hides and pieces of old canvas. At one time, nine people lived in the Tubbs dugout.

Tubbs and his brother-in-law Gus Carlisle were active in the founding of modern Lubbock. Before the city came into existence, two small villages—Lubbock and South Lubbock (Monterey)—vied for local leadership. Carlisle, who had convinced one of the founders, Whit Rayner, to come to Lubbock County, served as peacemaker. He brought the competing factions together,

Isham Tubbs was an early builder and successful entrepreneur in Lubbock. *Courtesy Sara Tubbs McKey.*

and they decided to combine their efforts and merge their villages at a new site—present downtown Lubbock.

For his part, Isham Tubbs traveled to Kentucky, where the owners of land proposed for the new town site lived. He convinced the absent landowners to sell 640 acres (a section) for the Lubbock project.

As part of the compromise for establishing the new town, Tubbs helped move many buildings and homes from Monterey and Lubbock to the new town site. He even helped move the large Nicolett Hotel, an early Lubbock landmark out near the present-day country club, to the town square.

An enterprising man, Tubbs, after a severe blizzard killed his cattle and ended his ranching venture, became an overland freighter. Before the arrival of railroads, most food, clothing, fuel, building materials and other necessities of life for area residents needed to be freighted to Lubbock from the nearest railroad stations: Colorado City and Amarillo. On each trip, Isham Tubbs hauled between two and three tons of supplies at a cost of one dollar per hundred pounds. A round trip to Amarillo or Colorado City took about two weeks.

To support his growing family, Tubbs found additional ways to earn a living. He and his sons caught mustangs, which were common on the Llano well into the 1900s, and broke them to ride. They sold many of them to the U.S. Army.

Later, he started a construction company, which fenced many area ranches. As the need to improve ranches and town lots continued, Tubbs and his sons expanded their business to include well drilling and windmill construction.

In 1908, the Tubbs family moved into a new home, a house built in the Queen Anne style, which was popular at the time. Texana, Tubbs's wife, chose the style after seeing a picture of a house she liked in a catalogue. Tubbs built the house large enough so that when all his children and grandchildren came for a visit, they could stay under one roof. After more than one hundred years, the house he built still stands on Lubbock's west side at Fulton Avenue, one block west of Frankfort and two blocks north of Fourth Street.

As one of the first men to move to the county, Tubbs worked on several early civic projects. He was a member of the first grand jury impaneled in Lubbock, served on the first county school board and became a founding member of the First United Methodist Church.

During his long life, Tubbs saw Lubbock grow from a small community of just thirty-three people to a thriving city of seventy thousand. He witnessed Lubbock's first train arrival in 1909, the expansion of the downtown business district, the establishment of Texas Technological College and the change of local agriculture from principally livestock raising to cotton growing.

Tubbs Elementary School, built in 1966 at 3311 Bates Street, is named in honor of Isham Tubbs.

Chapter 24

The "King Makers" of Lubbock

Paul H. Carlson

Political history and machinations in Lubbock are probably not much different than in other Texas and southern cities. But perhaps one way Lubbock was different was its mid-twentieth-century "empire builders" or "king makers" political clique. Something of an "old boy" network, its members influenced politics for nearly thirty years between the late 1930s and late 1960s. Indeed, the powerful cabal dominated Lubbock political life. Nearly always made up of men, the group often determined who would serve on the city council and who would be mayor. They did not always agree on the issues, but at election time, they usually supported their caucus's candidates.

The coterie met at a corner table—the "Round Table" it was called—on the mezzanine-level lunchroom or tearoom of Lubbock's finest downtown department store, Hemphill-Wells, at Thirteenth Street and Avenue J. Members met each day for lunch, but obviously with other matters, both personal and business, needing attention, they did not all sit together every day.

At the center of the circle were Charles "Charlie" Guy and Parker Prouty of the *Lubbock Avalanche Journal* and Alaric Brandt "A.B." Davis, one of the city's great chamber of commerce leaders.

Other members operated large, locally owned retail firms, including Roy Furr of the vast grocery store and cafeteria chain of Furr's Incorporated; Spencer Wells of Hemphill-Wells department store; and Retha and Ruel Martin of Dunlap's, another upscale department store.

The "king makers" met daily for lunch at Hemphill-Wells new department store, constructed in downtown Lubbock in 1950. *Courtesy Southwest Collection, Texas Tech University.*

The group also included Charles E. Maedgen of Lubbock National Bank, Walter Posey and Roy Riddle of First National Bank and, in the early days, Sam C. Arnett Sr. and George Benson of Citizens National Bank.

Similarly, leaders from three large downtown law firms sat at the Round Table. These included attorneys with Crenshaw, Dupree and Milam associated with First National Bank; Key, Carr and Carr allied with Lubbock National Bank; and Klett, Bean and Evans linked with Citizens National Bank.

Membership in the close-knit little group changed over time as people moved away, retired from active political life or died. But, writes Roger Schaefer, leaders of the downtown business, financial and legal institutions continued to meet each weekday for years. They talked about social and political issues, discussed future actions that would be best for Lubbock and, as city elections approached, decided on their candidates for political office. Between 1946 and 1964, Round Table candidates with the backing of the formidable Rotary Club of Lubbock won nearly every mayoral election. Jack Strong in 1962 represented the exception.

The king makers' success relates to their vigorous leadership, their control of the city's media outlets and perhaps especially to the "at large" political system that operated in Lubbock. Under it, candidates running for a place

One of the "king makers" was Charlie Guy (*left*), longtime editor of the *Lubbock Avalanche-Journal*, pictured here with former Texas Tech president Clifford B. Jones (*center*) and Byron Shotts, circa 1968. *Courtesy Southwest Collection, Texas Tech University.*

on the city council did not represent a specific district or area of the city. Instead, they represented the city at large—the entire city. The single-member system now in place did not begin until 1984.

Even before then, however, beginning in the mid-1960s, the Round Table group was losing its hold on Lubbock politics. For one thing, the city was growing in population and expanding away from its downtown core. People living south of Fiftieth Street and west of Indiana Avenue did not always share empire builder ideals. For another, African American and Mexican American citizens, who likewise did not always agree with the group's goals, began demanding a voice in their city's political life.

In the end, perhaps several developments doomed empire builder dominance. One of them included the long struggle of Lubbock racial and ethnic minority citizens to gain a greater voice in local government. They got it first by appointment to city boards and commissions and much later by winning election to political office.

A second was the so-called Homer Maxey Bank War involving financial, legal and real estate issues, plus some questionable banking ethics. Its struggles between Maxey, a millionaire city developer, and some new leaders of Citizens National Bank began in 1966. The long "war" shattered empire builder cohesion as members divided over the battle's complicated financial issues.

A third was the opening in 1972 of the South Plains Shopping Mall. It brought to Lubbock a number of outside vendors and national chain stores that competed with such local firms as Hemphill-Wells and Dunlap's. The homeownership structure began falling apart with the opening of the mall.

Nonetheless, the king makers should not be despised. Their cooperation and leadership secured Reese Air Force Base in the 1940s, helped to get Texas Technological College's sports programs into the prominent Southwest Conference, acquired for the city several new agriculture-related businesses in the 1950s, achieved better airport facilities and won other economic benefits in the 1960s. For nearly thirty years, they served Lubbock well.

Part IV
Legend Makers

This chapter is about legends that were created on or who have lived on or near the Llano Estacado. Included are some of the most important political, educational and cultural builders of the region. Elizabeth "Aunt Hank" Smith typified the pioneer woman, Bill Harrod fostered the development and growth of the Lubbock Symphony Orchestra and Governor Preston Smith gave the region an unprecedented boost through his long service in Texas politics.

To tell the story of all the legendary figures in the region would be quite a study in itself. Such a book would surely include such pioneers as the Causey brothers and Hank Smith. It would also tell about black cowboys "80 John" Wallace and Bones Hooks and strong-willed women like Mary Blankenship, Mamie Burns, Christine DeVitt and Helen Jones. It would include entertainers from the region such as Roy Orbison and Waylon Jennings, as well as longtime congressman George Mahon.

Already in this study, you have read of several notable legends, including George Singer, Mollie Abernathy, the Lady in Blue and Quanah Parker. The latter was probably the most legendary figure to cross the plains, rivaled only by his nemesis, Colonel Ranald Slidell Mackenzie. The legend of Mackenzie is well documented in the region by trails and place names, but as you will see, it was overshadowed by another on the national scene.

The part begins with the story of a nineteenth-century German novelist who, although he never visited the Llano Estacado, made it within the minds of his legions of fans into one of the most legendary places in the world.

Chapter 25

German Novelist Karl May and the Llano Estacado

Meredith McClain

In the late 1970s and the 1980s, young German backpackers coming to Lubbock often asked two questions: "*Wo ist der Buddy Holly Park?*" and "*Wo ist der Llano Estacado?*" Answering the first question was not a problem, but the second? Just where is the Llano Estacado?

Since the 1970s, several books have thoroughly defined and described the region of which Lubbock is the unofficial capital. In addition, weathermen and women now talk about "the weather on the Llano."

Still, I was unprepared for the response of an audience in Bonn, Germany, when, representing Texas Tech University, I introduced myself and said I came from Lubbock, Texas, "the capital of the Llano Estacado."

All the Germans in the room looked at me very intently. At the end of the program, many of them approached to say they thought people could not live on the Llano Estacado because there was so little water. They also mentioned "bad guys" riding about the desert, moving signs to water so people would go astray and die before being robbed.

One German took pity on me, saying, "Look up the writer Karl May."

Born in 1842, Karl Friedrich May was the fifth of fourteen children, nine of whom died in infancy. His father was a weaver. Although Karl performed well in school, his increasingly nefarious activities landed him in prison—twice.

Sometime after his second prison experience, May became an editor at Müchmeyer Press in Saxony, his home state. Starting there, and then without ever leaving Germany, he wrote western adventure stories in the first person.

German writer Karl May.
Wikimedia Commons.

He set four of the novels on the Llano Estacado, and in them and other books he described the American Southwest.

So convincing were his descriptions that his readers—mainly young boys and girls—knew that he, Karl, was Charlie, the German frontiersman, aka "Old Shatterhand," blood-brother of the handsome, wise and honorable Mescalero Apache Chief Winnetou. The two popular characters rode from one thrilling adventure to the next on the dangerous Llano Estacado. The stories became best-selling novels.

In later years, revelations that May had never been to the Llano created minor scandals. Adult fans felt betrayed after they discovered that for personal appearances as Old Shatterhand, May dressed in "western" outfits created in Germany and used guns crafted in Dresden.

Children did not mind, and when not allowed to peruse May's writings, they went under the bedcovers with flashlights to read his "forbidden" books, one dog-eared copy after another. Winnetou and Old Shatterhand became household words throughout the German-speaking world.

Near the end of World War II, purportedly, Karl May and his heroes of the American West became signals for German soldiers. If he heard someone approaching his position, a German soldier, worried it might be an American, whispered, "Karl May." "Winnetou" was the coded answer.

May's growing success worldwide got an enormous boost in the 1960s. During the decade, West German filmmakers in communistic Yugoslavia turned several Winnetou stories into movies. Most starred Lex Barker (who also played Tarzan) as handsome, invincible Old Shatterhand, riding beside Winnetou, played by a Frenchman, Pierre Brice. In the movies, Serbo-Croatians played Native American parts.

Karl May died in 1912. A wealthy businessman, he never set foot on the Texas High Plains but nonetheless contributed in various ways to the mystique of the Llano Estacado.

Today, May is the best-selling German language author, having sold an estimated 100 million copies of his books in German and 100 million in about fifty other languages.

There are hundreds of western and Indian clubs throughout the Republic of Germany (one being "Lubbock Town" outside Cologne), at least seven outdoor theaters presenting May's stories and a Karl May Society, which had almost reached its goal of two thousand members worldwide when it held a conference in Lubbock in September 2000.

In about 1983, Professor Theodore Alexander, founder of the department of Germanic and Slavic Languages at Texas Tech, said that after escaping Adolph Hitler's takeover of Austria in the late 1930s, he landed safely in America. He came to Lubbock looking for the fantasy land of his childhood—Karl May's *der Llano Estacado*.

Chapter 26

Thomas S. Lubbock—Namesake of Lubbock County

David J. Murrah

The Texas legislature named Lubbock County in 1876 when it created fifty-four new counties in the Panhandle and South Plains. Most of the county names honored men who died at the Alamo or were signers of the Texas Declaration of Independence, veterans of the Battle of San Jacinto or early Texas pioneers. Three of the counties were named for service in the Civil War. Of the three, one was named for General Thomas J. "Stonewall" Jackson, who was not a Texan. The others were for two of Texas's most revered war heroes: Frank Terry and Thomas Saltus Lubbock.

Born in 1817 into a genteel merchant family in Charleston, South Carolina, young Tom Lubbock (correctly pronounced *Lub-bock*, not *Lub-bic*) grew up amid the fiery rhetoric of South Carolina's states' rights politics. Tough, proud and obstinate as a youth, he quit school and moved to New Orleans in early 1835.

In the city, Lubbock found much talk of Texas. He joined the New Orleans Grays, the first group of volunteers from the United States to enter the fray for an independent Texas. Tom and the Grays arrived in Texas in November 1835. They joined 250 other Texans and drove the Mexican army temporarily out of San Antonio.

Lubbock remained in the village a few more weeks, but after becoming ill, he left for East Texas. The sickness probably saved his life, as many of his compatriots died shortly afterward at the Alamo.

Tom, as he returned eastward, stumbled into an old family friend operating a steamboat on the Colorado River. The friend nursed Lubbock back to

The city of Lubbock and Lubbock County are named for former Texas Ranger and Civil War hero Tom S. Lubbock. *Wikimedia Commons.*

health and gave him employment. While working on the boat, Tom helped ferry Sam Houston's army across the Colorado River and ducked shots fired by Mexican soldiers trying to capture the craft.

Later, Lubbock arrived at San Jacinto with the Texas government. It was four days after Houston's glorious victory. Tom vowed that he would not miss such action again.

Thus, in 1841, Lubbock joined the ill-fated Santa Fe Expedition, an attempt by Texas to extend its jurisdiction over eastern New Mexico and part of present-day Colorado. While heading toward Santa Fe, the expedition became lost in western Texas, abandoned much of its equipment and floundered trying to ascend the Llano Estacado's escarpment northeast of present-day Lubbock. Harassed by Indians and suffering other hardships, the expedition fell apart. It eventually surrendered to a Mexican force, but Tom Lubbock had passed within sixty miles of the county that was later to bear his name.

Mexican officials marched the captured Texans to Mexico City and imprisoned them. Shortly afterward, Lubbock escaped by jumping from a balcony. He hid for a few weeks in Mexico City and then, with the aid of friends, made his way back to Texas.

He became a cotton dealer in Houston. In December 1843, he married Sarah Obedience Smith, and between 1844 and 1858, the couple reared seven children.

After the presidential election of Abraham Lincoln, Tom Lubbock led Harris County in 1861 in the fight for secession from the United States. With the outbreak of the Civil War, he and his close friend Frank Terry hastened to the Confederate capital to seek permission to raise troops for the South. Their request denied, the pair returned to Texas briefly and then hurried to Virginia, determined to fight as guerrillas if necessary. They joined General James Longstreet's command and won recognition for bravery in scouting enemy movements at the Battle of Manassas (First Battle of Bull Run).

Their battlefield performance got them permission to organize a Texas cavalry force. Returning home in August 1861, Terry and Lubbock quickly raised the volunteer companies that became known as Terry's Texas Rangers.

The next month, the unit left Texas bound for Virginia, but it diverted to Kentucky and into immediate action. Early in its first skirmish, occurring in December 1861, the commander, Frank Terry, died in action. The men chose Lubbock to replace him, but Tom, very ill, was unable to assume his command. He died of typhus on January 9, 1862, in Nashville, Tennessee.

Tom's death was widely mourned in Texas. Soon after, a family friend wrote a lengthy poem that contained these two lines:

O Peaceful Lubbock be thy rest!
Thine is a name "not born to die."

Little did the poet realize how true his words were, for a county and city soon developed to ensure that Tom Lubbock's name was "not born to die."

Chapter 27

Mackenzie and Custer

David J. Murrah

A previous essay in this book on the Mackenzie Trail noted how famous the Mackenzie name is in Lubbock and across portions of the South Plains, memorialized by city and area landmarks, such as Mackenzie Park and the Mackenzie Reservoir near Tulia. These places honor Ranald Slidell Mackenzie, a highly successful U.S. cavalry officer who played a decisive role in ending the Indian wars on the Great Plains. His name, however, is hardly recognized outside Texas, and nationally it is shrouded by the shadow of one of his contemporaries, George Armstrong Custer. Custer's name adorns counties in seven different states and several towns in the Midwest. A national cemetery in Montana, a large state park in the Black Hills and a monument at West Point also bear his name.

The two, Mackenzie and Custer, are literally side by side in the annals of military history. At West Point, their names are listed together, as Custer graduated *last* in his class in 1861 and Mackenzie *first* in the class of 1862. Time and events proved Mackenzie to be the smarter and better officer, one who found himself having to clean up messes left by Custer.

Yet it was Custer's story that captured national attention. A recent Internet search cited more than two thousand books related to Custer, while Mackenzie appears in only twenty-eight. There have been at least thirty-two movies made about Custer and none about Mackenzie—although in 1958 and 1959, a television series, *Mackenzie's Raiders*, featured him.

Mackenzie was born in New York City in 1840 into a prominent American family. After his West Point education, he fought in the Civil War. During

Left to right: George Armstrong Custer, 1865, and Ranald Mackenzie, 1876. *Custer photo courtesy Library of Congress; Mackenzie photo from* Ranald S. Mackenzie on the Texas Frontier *by Ernest Wallace.*

it, he was wounded six times but each time quickly returned to service. By war's end, he had been appointed brevet major general of U.S. Volunteers. Mackenzie was only twenty-four.

After a brief stint in civilian life, Mackenzie in 1866 returned to the military and by 1871 had become commander of the Fourth Cavalry, stationed at Fort Concho at present-day San Angelo. Over the next three years, he distinguished himself in several battles, including the decisive skirmish in September 1874 in Palo Duro Canyon, which brought an end to the Red River War.

George Custer also distinguished himself during the Civil War but in its aftermath faced near mutiny by his troops while serving in Texas in late 1865. In 1866, aided by his political connections, Custer became commander of the Seventh Cavalry, stationed at Fort Riley, Kansas. In November 1868, his troops attacked the Cheyenne winter encampment of Black Kettle on the Washita River in Oklahoma, resulting in immediate debate as to whether it was a battle or massacre.

In 1873, the army sent the Seventh Cavalry to the Dakotas, where Custer soon came into conflict with the Sioux. Determined to win a glorious battle to help him become president of the United States, Custer met his death at Little Big Horn on June 25, 1876, when his entire command of 208 men was wiped out by more than 1,000 warriors.

After the debacle at Little Big Horn, the army sent Mackenzie and the Fourth Cavalry to the northern plains to clean up the mess. There, in November 1876, only five months after Custer's ignominious defeat, they overwhelmed a northern Cheyenne band led by Dull Knife.

Mackenzie's victory helped to bring an end to the Black Hills War. Custer's death brought him long-sought and lasting fame. Mackenzie's demise did just the opposite. His death was tragic but quiet. He had been promoted to brigadier general in 1882, but by that time, his physical and mental health had deteriorated significantly, and in 1884, he retired from the military. He died without fanfare in 1889 at age forty-eight.

Why is the flamboyant Custer more famous than Mackenzie? One obvious answer lies in the nature of their deaths. Custer "died with his boots on," a part of a highly publicized campaign in the midst of the country's centennial celebration. Mackenzie, mentally ill and often hospitalized, simply faded away.

Another answer is found in the words of the late military historian Charles Kenner, who summarized it this way: he said that Mackenzie was "the most uniformly successful and least publicized Indian fighter of the 1870s... almost the exact antithesis of the least successful and most publicized—George Custer."

According to Kenner, Custer "specialized in penning lengthy, self-serving, and bombastic descriptions of his campaigns [whereas] Mackenzie was exasperatingly terse." Moreover, Mackenzie left no memoirs and little correspondence. As a result, Custer remains famous today in large part because of the "amount of grist left for the historian's mill."

Chapter 28

Elizabeth Boyle "Aunt Hank" Smith

Paul H. Carlson

Elizabeth Boyle Smith (1848–1925), sometimes called "the mother of the plains," was the first permanent Anglo woman on the South Plains. Born in Scotland, Elizabeth Boyle came with three of her brothers to America when she was between eighteen and twenty years old. They settled with a fourth brother already living in Missouri.

A few years later, Elizabeth's brothers determined to go west. They headed for Texas, moving to communities near Fort Griffin on the frontier in Shackelford County, places considered among the "toughest" in the state. Elizabeth, at least temporarily, stayed behind, but upon her mother's death in Scotland, her father joined her in Missouri. Not long afterward, in December 1873, Elizabeth and her father followed her brothers to Texas. They traveled by train to Dallas and then on board a stagecoach rode to Fort Worth, where her brother James, a druggist, met them. James took them in an ox-drawn wagon to Fort Griffin, a trip that took a week.

On December 31, at a New Year's Eve dance that W. Hubert Curry called "an old-fashioned rollicking breakdown…attended by cowboys [from] miles around and officers" from the nearby military instillation, Elizabeth met Henry Clay "Hank" Smith. Hank, a cowboy, sailor, Civil War veteran, teamster and entrepreneur, had recently acquired a contract to supply the post at Fort Griffin with hay and wood. Their chance meeting became instant love. Hank, Elizabeth said, came to see her every Sunday for a while and then twice a week. They married on May 19, 1874; she was twenty-six, Hank thirty-eight.

Elizabeth "Aunt Hank" and Hank Smith, circa 1902. *Courtesy Southwest Collection, Texas Tech University.*

Over the next several years, the couple had six children: Henry, who died five months after his May 1875 birth; George, born in 1876; Leila, born in 1878; Robert, born in 1881; Annie, born in 1883; and Mary, born in 1887.

A year or so after their marriage, Elizabeth and Hank took over management of the Occidental Hotel at Fort Griffin, a structure Hank built in 1875 and that Curry called "the best hostelry west of Fort Worth."

Because her husband was often gone on business, Elizabeth, or "Aunt Hank," as she was beginning to be called, took major responsibility for operation of the hotel. In such a capacity, she became acquainted with public officials, cowboys and cattlemen, soldiers, lawyers and many travelers. The associations, her granddaughter said, "continued uninterrupted almost to the closing days of her life and made her one of the best loved women in the entire state."

At the hotel, Aunt Hank, with "knowledge of fine cooking," writes Curry, became a famous hostess. In the hotel's dining room, she showed off "her silverware, silver service, cutware and fine china received at her wedding" but used it only on Sundays.

In November 1878, the couple moved west to Blanco Canyon in upper Crosby County, where Hank Smith had taken over a failed cattle ranch. At the ranch, Smith between 1877 and 1878 had supervised the final construction of a large two-story stone house, and in this "Rock House," as it would be called, Aunt Hank made a home for her growing family.

The Smiths operated a store at the new home, and while Hank ran cattle and sheep and grew several different kinds of crops, Aunt Hank, beginning in 1879, became postmistress. She ran the post office Mount Blanco Station, located a few yards from the Rock House, for thirty-nine years—until 1916.

Aunt Hank, according to Phoebe K. Warner, also "taught the first school on the South Plains." She instructed her children and later some neighbors' children in the Rock House.

Warner also writes that Aunt Hank "always kept an upstairs room" in her home "just for sick cowboys and travelers." She was both doctor and nurse. In fact, she had learned some basic medicine while helping physicians and surgeons at Fort Griffin. And before leaving for Blanco Canyon, she convinced doctors to supply her with a large batch of medicines.

In Blanco Canyon, Aunt Hank became a good friend of Mrs. H.H. Campbell, whose husband managed the large Matador Ranch about sixty miles away. Other early friends included Mrs. W.C. Dockum, who lived on a ranch about twenty miles away; Mrs. John H. Jacobs, who helped manage the store at Mount Blanco; and, after 1879, the Quaker settlers at nearby Estacado.

Food was plentiful. Aunt Hank raised garden vegetables and picked wild plums, grapes and nuts with her children. In addition to beef and mutton, her husband provided deer, pronghorn and other wild game—even bison in the first year they lived in the canyon.

Elizabeth Boyle "Aunt Hank" Smith was a homemaker, nurse, postmistress, schoolteacher and hostess for a large number of visitors and, writes Warner, "a mother to everyone who crossed her threshold." She was independent and self-reliant, and after her husband's death in 1912, she continued to operate the ranch Glorietta Hacienda for several more years.

Aunt Hank died in 1925 and is buried in Crosby County's Emma Cemetery.

Chapter 29

Bill Harrod and the Lubbock Symphony Orchestra

Curtis Peoples

The year 2016 marked the seventieth anniversary of the Lubbock Symphony Orchestra (LSO). The LSO began after World War II, when serviceman and musician Bill Harrod, who had been stationed in Lubbock, decided to settle there.

William Harrod was born in Des Moines, Iowa, in 1913. He spent his childhood in Little Rock, Arkansas. Harrod's paternal side of the family all had a musical background. Harrod's father played with John Philip Sousa and his older brother with the Dorsey brothers. When he was in New York, Harrod played with Jimmy Durante and at times was on the highly popular Jack Benny radio program. He spent many years in New York studying violin as a pupil of Andor Schoen and Emanuel Zetlin.

After World War II started, Harrod joined the army, and in 1942 and 1943, he was stationed at Lubbock Army Airfield. He then went overseas for an extensive tour of Europe as the director of a string quartet playing mainly at army hospitals. After his service, he returned to Lubbock and married Audrey Johnson.

Other cities in the region, like Amarillo, Abilene and Roswell, for years had seasoned community orchestras. During Lubbock's early history, small orchestras formed from time to time, but none was long lasting.

The idea for a permanent Lubbock symphony did not come into fruition until the spring of 1946. In May, Mrs. M.C. Butler, a member of the Park and Recreation Planning Committee, advanced the symphony idea at a joint program-planning meeting. The goal was to develop an orchestra similar

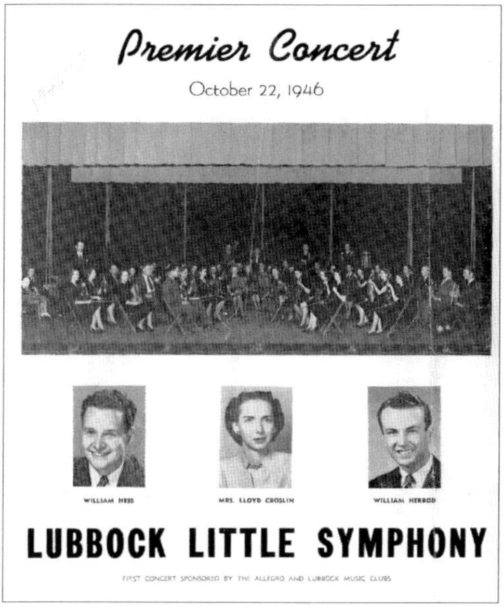

Program brochure for the first concert of what later became the Lubbock Symphony Orchestra. The cover featured William Hess (*left*), Mrs. Lloyd Croslin and William Harrod, founder of the Symphony. *Courtesy Curtis Peoples.*

to other civic orchestras. It would hold concerts with guest soloists and give local musicians a chance to perform with the group. To win support for the orchestra, Harrod contacted several local religious leaders and, as a result, found himself playing at many Sunday night church services. The Parks and Recreation Department allocated $100 for the program and sought a trial period for the orchestra during the summer. At the close of the summer, the symphony was to play a concert as a preview to a fall and winter series.

Accordingly, at the local USO building on June 10, 1946, the symphony held its first rehearsal. Bill Harrod volunteered his services as the conductor of the fledgling orchestra. Local musicians who joined him included Julian K. Blitz, D.O. Wiley, Louis Stoelzing and Beverly Vaughn. In all, about thirty-five people attended the rehearsal. Miss Leona Gelin volunteered to serve as the symphony's business manager. From the first, Harrod lobbied to have the musicians paid, but it remained a volunteer organization until 1967.

In its early years, the lack of string players was an obstacle for the symphony. Brass and woodwind players had been trained well in the Lubbock public school system or at Texas Technological College. Harrod said, "The thing that kept us going early on was the Texas Tech band and its wonderful musicians." Although there was an abundance of band members, the orchestra began with only a "scrub team of fiddle players." Partly, as a result, rehearsals concentrated on strings.

On July 1, 1946, during its fourth rehearsal, the symphony held a practice concert that received enthusiastic public approval. As a result, an executive board formed to encourage the continuation of the organization.

Dubbed the Lubbock Little Symphony, its premiere concert was held on October 22, 1946, in the Lubbock High School auditorium. The Allegro and Lubbock Music Clubs sponsored the concert. Headliners included Bill Harrod, William Hess and Mrs. Lloyd Croslin.

Harrod gave credit to Nat Williams, superintendent of Lubbock Independent School District, for "turning things around musically" in the city. He said that Williams announced that he wanted schools to have an orchestra teacher as well as a band teacher.

Harrod found the local orchestra teachers to be good players and recruited them. He also said that the orchestra received its biggest blessing in violinist Virginia Kellogg. After her arrival, he believed, the organization started sounding like a real orchestra.

Other Lubbock citizens he credited with playing major roles in the development of the orchestra were Asher Thompson and Charley Pope. Harrod said there was always a good local audience for the orchestra. People wanted things to do.

In the 1940s in Lubbock, conducting an orchestra was not considered a profession. Therefore, Harrod opened a music store. He said that people were always good to his family, and so it was a happy life in Lubbock. William Harrod died on January 1, 2011, in Tampa Bay, Florida.

Chapter 30

Buddy Holly

Curtis Peoples

The youngest of four children, Charles Hardin "Buddy" Holley was born in Lubbock on September 7, 1936, to Lawrence Odel "L.O." and Ella Holley. His family nicknamed him Buddy.

Growing up in a musical family, Buddy was encouraged to play music and performed in his first show at the age of five. Although throughout his youth he learned to play various instruments, he eventually settled on the guitar as his instrument of choice.

While attending Hutchison Junior High School, Buddy began to take music seriously when he partnered with his friend Bob Montgomery. Billed as "Buddy and Bob," the duo performed bluegrass and country songs. Buddy and Bob played at many local functions and eventually on the KDAV radio station show *The Sunday Party*.

Throughout his junior high and high school years, Buddy also teamed with other area musicians, including Sonny Curtis, Larry Welborn, Don Guess, Jack Neal and others. One might have seen one of these early combos playing at Lawson's Skating Rink, Sewell's Country Market, teen clubs or opening for touring musical acts.

Early musical influences on Holley included not only bluegrass and country but also rhythm and blues. According to Jack Neal, Buddy liked to hear local African American R&B musicians in small cafés on Lubbock's east side. Late at night, Buddy listened to his favorite artists on such radio stations as KWKH in Shreveport, Louisiana.

Buddy Holly and the Crickets, 1957, including Jerry Allison (*top*), Buddy Holly and Joe B. Mauldin. *Wikimedia Commons.*

In 1955, Buddy's musical world changed. He saw Elvis Presley perform rock-and-roll music, and the new form became his calling.

In early 1956, Holley began his professional recording career in Nashville for Decca Records. He released four sides, or two double-sided discs, on Decca Records. On the initial release, the company misspelled Buddy's last name on the records as Holly. The name stuck.

Due to poor record sales and lack of creative control, Holly sought a new record deal. Thus, he began recording with Norman Petty in Clovis, New Mexico. Petty had success producing and promoting records, and in 1957, the partnership proved fruitful when Buddy and his band scored a hit with "That'll Be the Day."

Known as The Crickets, with Buddy Holly on vocal and lead guitar, Jerry Allison on drums, Joe B. Mauldin on bass and Niki Sullivan on rhythm guitar, the group toured the United States. Their self-titled debut album *The "Chirping" Crickets* was released on November 27, 1957.

The Crickets continued to release hit records like "Peggy Sue," "Oh Boy," "Not Fade Away," "Words of Love," "Listen to Me," "Love's Made a Fool of You," "Maybe Baby" and "Everyday." The group made television appearances on *Arthur Murray's Dance Party*, *American Bandstand* and the *Ed Sullivan Show*. In early 1958, Buddy had a return engagement on the *Ed Sullivan Show* and toured Hawaii, Australia and the United Kingdom. His debut solo album, *Buddy Holly*, was released in February 1958.

In 1958, major changes occurred for Holly. During a visit to the Peermusic offices in New York City, he met Maria Elena Santiago. After a whirlwind romance, the two were married on August 15, 1958, and settled in New York.

Later that year, Holly returned to Petty Studios to record, but fractures in his partnerships with Petty and The Crickets began to emerge. In December, he split from Petty and The Crickets.

With his finances tied up in litigation and in need of money, Holly decided to go out on tour and formed a new band with Waylon Jennings on electric bass, Tommy Allsup on guitar and Carl Bunch on drums.

Billed as the Winter Dance Party, Buddy Holly, Dion and the Belmonts, Ritchie Valens and the Big Bopper began a tour of the Midwest, with their opening show in Milwaukee on January 23, 1959. The tour was plagued with logistical problems and freezing weather.

After their show in Clear Lake, Iowa, on February 3, 1959, Buddy chartered a plane to fly himself, Jennings and Allsup to the next stop in Moorhead, Minnesota. Instead, Ritchie Valens and the Big Bopper accompanied Holly on the flight. Shortly after takeoff in cold and snowy weather, the plane crashed, killing all three musicians and the pilot, Roger Peterson.

Although his career was short, Buddy Holly's musical sway is monumental. His music influenced the Beatles, the Rolling Stones, Bob Dylan and countless others. He had planned to open his own recording studio in Lubbock. His imprint on popular music continues to this day.

The City of Lubbock in 1999 opened the Buddy Holly Center, where visitors can learn more about Buddy Holly and see artifacts related to the pioneering musician. Many scholars agree that his music and impact will "Not Fade Away."

Chapter 31

GOVERNOR PRESTON SMITH

Donald Walker

Preston Smith (1912–2003) enjoyed a long and varied career in public life. In November 1944, when he was thirty-two years old, he won the first of three consecutive terms in the Texas House of Representatives. Smith lost his race for lieutenant governor in 1950 but six years later won a seat in the Texas Senate. He was reelected in 1960, and two years later, voters chose him for the first of three consecutive terms as lieutenant governor, the most powerful position in state government. The culmination of his political career came in 1968, when he won election to the first of two terms as Texas governor.

Voters of the state always associated Smith with the northwest Texas districts he represented in Austin, but in point of fact, he was a native of central Texas, having been born on a small farm near Georgetown in Williamson County. Smith was one of thirteen children, and when he was eleven in 1923, the family left central Texas and moved to Dawson County on the Texas High Plains. He finished Lamesa High School in 1930, entered Texas Tech in the fall and graduated with a degree in business in 1934. Shortly thereafter, he married his college sweetheart, Ima Smith of Ralls, thus forging a union that lasted the remainder of their lives and produced two children, Mickey and Jan.

Early in his first term in the legislature, Smith determined to take an active role in the legislative process. He introduced a bill that would have dissolved the Permanent University Fund (PUF), that very large pool of money that came from exploiting oil beneath certain state-owned lands.

Statute dictated that those monies should be reserved for the exclusive use of the University of Texas and Texas A&M. Smith challenged the existing system by substituting for it an arrangement that would divide the money among all the public institutions in accordance with the number of students each institution enrolled. Very simply stated, he believed that all Texas youngsters attending a public college or university in Texas should benefit from the monies derived from state lands. The bill generated a firestorm of controversy, as supporters of UT and A&M used every tool available to prevent an open public vote on the measure. The bill eventually failed, but Smith won in the sense that he brought much-needed public attention to the issue of fair and equitable funding for all higher education in Texas.

Over his career, Smith consistently fought to expand educational opportunities for all Texas youngsters, and his years as lieutenant governor and later as governor provide clear evidence of the extent to which his efforts made a profound difference. From the lieutenant governor's office, Smith secured legislative approval for Texas Tech to establish a law school. During his years as governor, Smith oversaw the opening of seven new community colleges, nine new branch campuses of four-year universities, a new dental school in San Antonio and two new medical colleges—the University of Texas Medical School at Houston and the Texas Tech University School of Medicine in Lubbock.

The Preston Smith statue in the courtyard of the Texas Tech University Administration Building. *Courtesy Monte Monroe.*

Smith took particular pride in the establishment of institutions that would support vocational training already being provided by the state's high schools and community colleges. Subsequently, the Texas State Technical Institute, which opened in Waco in 1969, grew to include campuses in Amarillo, Harlingen and Sweetwater. Enrollments at each of the four schools greatly exceeded expectations. It was for very good reason that many persons familiar with Texas state government in the years after World War II often referred to Smith as "the education governor."

Shortly after his retirement from public life, a group of Smith's friends and supporters around the state began a campaign to erect a permanent memorial to him. The group included people who understood and appreciated the extent and significance of the work he had done to further education. From their efforts came the larger-than-life statue of Smith on the campus of Texas Tech University. Located in the courtyard of the administration building, the statue serves as a permanent reminder of the contributions Smith made to our state and region throughout his lengthy political career.

Dolph Briscoe, who succeeded Smith as governor, remembered Smith as a public official who "was devoted to Lubbock, West Texas, and Texas Tech." In Briscoe's opinion, Smith, more than anyone else, "built Texas Tech into the great institution of higher learning that it is today."

Chapter 32

Lauro Cavazos of Texas Tech

Gene B. Preuss

There is nothing so uniquely Texan as Santa Gertrudis cattle, the Brahman-Shorthorn cross named for the Spanish land grant that Richard King acquired to build his South Texas ranching empire. For many years, the acknowledged expert on those cattle was Lauro Cavazos Sr., the first Mexican-American foreman of the King Ranch.

Although Cavazos and his wife, Tomasa, had minimal formal education, they made sure their children were well educated. The children began school at a two-room schoolhouse on the ranch, but Lauro soon moved the family to the nearby town of Kingsville, where, upon his insistence, they attended Flato school, an Anglo institution. It was a difficult request and transition for a Mexican-American family in South Texas to make in the 1930s. In the period prior to school desegregation, most Mexican-Americans in South Texas were compelled by local custom to attend separate Mexican schools. Yet because of Cavazos's standing in the community, the school superintendent agreed to the request, and the Cavazos children became the first Mexican-Americans to attend the white school. They did not stop there.

"My father had three requirements," Lauro Cavazos Jr. once explained. "He said we should get all the education we could; he said we should serve our community; and he said we should honor the family name."

Although their father died in 1958, the Cavazos children followed their parents' code. Sarita Cavazos Ochoa taught public school for nearly four decades. Her brother Robert, or "Bobby," attended Texas Tech and was a running back on the football team, becoming one of the most decorated

Dr. Lauro F. Cavazos, circa 1988. *Courtesy Southwest Collection, Texas Tech University.*

players in Tech's history. After serving in the U.S. Army in the Korean conflict, he became a foreman at the King Ranch and, like his father before him, served as a county commissioner in Kingsville. Another brother, Richard, also attended Tech and became a career military officer, serving in Korea and Vietnam. He later became the first Hispanic four-star general, and he also served as a regent for Texas Tech. The youngest Cavazos, Joseph, served as an executive for Sears Roebuck & Company.

Lauro Jr., the subject of this essay, completed his undergraduate and master's degrees at Texas Tech and earned a PhD in physiology from Iowa State University. He married Peggy Murdock, a nurse from Littlefield whom he had met in Lubbock.

After teaching and becoming a higher education administrator, Lauro Cavazos Jr. in 1980 returned to Texas Tech, where he became the first Mexican-American and first alumnus to serve as the university's president. "As you can imagine, this is a moving experience for me," he told the audience at his installation, "to be inaugurated as president of an institution for which I have long held the deepest affection and respect."

Cavazos often returned to his parents' advice in his public speeches. In 1981, he told a gathering of the League of United Latin American Citizens in Corpus Christi, "I remember my father saying, 'Son, educate yourself. An education is the most valuable thing you can have. It is the one thing that no one can ever take away from you.'"

In 1988, President Ronald Reagan named Cavazos secretary of education, the first Mexican-American to serve in a cabinet position. He continued the position under President George H.W. Bush until 1990.

Reagan, who had once called the Department of Education a "bureaucratic boondoggle," eventually came to see the importance of the federal role in education. Building on the momentum for educational reform by the publication of *A Nation at Risk*, Cavazos expanded that trend. Furthermore, Cavazos and the state governors laid the foundation for national education standards. Finally, he began calling for better educational service for minority students, especially Hispanics, who suffered from high dropout rates.

Cavazos often reminded his audiences of Thomas Jefferson's admonition: "If a nation expects to be ignorant and free in a state of civilization, it expects what never was and never will be."

Even after he left Washington, D.C., Cavazos continued to advocate for educational reform and the importance of education for everyone. As part of that effort, Texas Tech University Press recently released his memoirs, *A Kineño's Journey: On Family, Learning, and Public Service.*

After retirement, Cavazos and his wife, Peggy, continue to split their time between their homes in Massachusetts and Texas. Dedication and hard work were hallmarks of the Cavazos family's success, and they are clearly demonstrated in the life and work of Texas Tech's Lauro Cavazos.

Part V
Tough Times

If you live in West Texas, you certainly know about how the weather can change instantly—sometimes for only a day but, especially in the case of drought, potentially for years. This section focuses, in part, on extremes of weather by remembering two horrendous sandstorms, a surprising flood and the deadly May 11, 1970 Lubbock tornado.

In the early 1900s, trains brought thousands of prospective settlers to the region and hastened the colonization of the Llano Estacado. This part includes two stories that tell of the rise and fall of two unique places in the region, Soash and Three Way, two communities that developed primarily from land sale promotions. Soash failed due to drought, and Three Way due to paved roads and farm mechanization.

One story relates to one of the darkest days ever for the region, when members of the Ku Klux Klan tarred and feathered the Catholic priest in Slaton. Another tells about the time when Abilene lost its bid to get a major state college, a loss that eventually became Lubbock's greatest day ever.

Chapter 33

W.P. Soash and Excursion Trains to the South Plains

Jennifer Spurrier

In the early twentieth century, town promoters and land agents like William Pulver Soash used railroad excursion trains to introduce potential midwestern settlers and farmers to property on the South Plains. That is, they arranged visits onboard Pullman train cars to give buyers a chance to look over available land.

Soash, who was from Iowa and one of the best-known such developers, purchased part of the giant XIT Ranch lands. He then contracted for excursion trains to Dalhart in the northwestern Panhandle of Texas. The trains brought land seekers from the Midwest, and after they debarked, Soash arranged for the travelers to be taken in buggies or early automobiles to see the available land. Buyers at first stayed onboard the trains. But Soash built a hotel at Ware, north of Dalhart, where new arrivals were closer to land the promoter was selling.

Soash soon became acquainted with C.C. Slaughter. Thereupon, he sold his interest in the land around Dalhart, established in Iowa the W.P. Soash Land Company and purchased a part of Slaughter's Running Water Ranch land in Lamb County, northwest of Lubbock.

Because a rural post office existed near the land he wanted to sell, Soash convinced the postmaster to move the office to a town site he was promoting. The town became Olton, and Soash assisted with getting a bank and church started. Olton was located near a railway line, and Soash ran excursion trains into the locale. Eventually, he sold about 100,000 acres in the region.

Iowa land salesman W.P. Soash perfected the use of excursion trains to bring prospective buyers to the High Plains. This train came from the Midwest to Dalhart in 1906. *Courtesy Southwest Collection, Texas Tech University.*

In 1909, Soash entered into a second agreement with Slaughter. This one included lands that were part of the Long S Ranch, divisions of which were in Borden, Dawson, Howard and Martin Counties.

Big Spring stood near the heart of the region, and in 1909, Soash began running excursion trains there. The first train came from Minneapolis to Fort Worth via the Rock Island Railway and then from Fort Worth to Big Spring via the Texas and Pacific line. Citizens of Big Spring heartily welcomed the newly arriving land seekers.

Soash also felt strongly enough about the area that he began the town of Soash, just north of Big Spring. He built a hotel, a bank and his home, and he moved the W.P. Soash Land Company's main office from Iowa to Soash.

Developers like W.P. Soash often used promotional brochures to attract buyers. A land promotion brochure issued in 1912 by the Atchison, Topeka and Santa Fe Railroad, for example, contains a vivid description of the Panhandle and the South Plains. The brochure includes a description of the region's climate, details about what crops can be grown and specifics about what livestock can be raised, as well as data on county populations, education and land value.

In one of his promotional brochures called *The Big Springs Country*, Soash wrote, "We have made arrangements for the establishment in Soash of a cotton gin, creamery, three churches, cement block factory, and a two-story school building has been completed and school is now in session." The brochure, distributed throughout the Midwest, included details about an excursion train he had organized. "You will travel in comfort on our own Special train composed of Buffet, Library Car, Standard Pullmans and Diner," it said. "It's a trip you'll remember all your life—to a country of abounding resources and unlimited possibilities."

Trains, the document indicated, would run the first and third Tuesdays of each month. Soash later stated that on one excursion out of Kansas City, "our train consisted of two engines and fourteen standard sleepers, with 240 some home seekers on board."

Most trains, he said years later, "averaged from 75 to 150" would-be settlers. Soash's "special trains" carried to Texas about 10,000 people.

The town of Soash did not last. From 1909 to 1912, the area suffered a long drought, and the town lacked a railroad. The combination doomed Soash, his company and his land-sales operations.

However, the promoters and even railroads continued to use excursion trains. The Santa Fe Railroad offered reduced ticket prices and other incentives to get people to Amarillo and the South Plains. Twice a month at the Santa Fe depot in Amarillo, realtors and land developers provided fancy Pope-Toledo touring cars to take home seekers across the prairies.

An urban legend says that while he was a high school student, Ernest O. Thompson, later mayor of Amarillo, saved money, bought a Pope-Toledo and every second Friday skipped school to haul prospective settlers into the country. His teachers complained of his absence, the story goes, but he made more money each Friday than his teachers did in a month.

World War I closed most such activities, but even before then, W.P. Soash's land company, his namesake town and his part in the excursion train promotions had ended.

Chapter 34

The Aborted West Texas A&M, 1917

David J. Murrah

Had it not been for a rascal for a governor, Texas Tech might not have existed. It is a story that began about a hundred years ago, when, in 1916, residents of the Panhandle and South Plains were barnstorming for a new college for West Texas.

Thanks to the world war raging in far-off Europe, West Texas was growing in population and wealth that year, with cotton selling for thirty cents a pound and wheat headed for two dollars a bushel.

Early that year, the secretary of the Amarillo Board of City Development, Porter Whaley, issued a call for regional cooperation in trying to get the state to establish a West Texas A&M college. The idea was not new. In 1910, the *Lubbock Avalanche* editor, J.J. Dillard, had called for the establishment of an "A&M on the plains" after Lubbock failed to secure getting the West Texas Normal College, which had been placed in Canyon in 1909. While Whaley may have been more motivated by trying to get a major college for Amarillo, which had also been passed over for the teachers' college, his appeal attracted a strong response, as fifty communities sent delegates to a planning conference that met in Sweetwater in April 1916. The group formed the West Texas A&M College Campaign Committee and secured monetary pledges from several cities, including Amarillo, Plainview and Lubbock.

The committee worked quickly and by early 1917 had persuaded the Texas legislature to pass a bill that created what was supposed to become the West Texas A&M College, to be located somewhere in Greater West

Texas's populist governor, James E. "Pa" Ferguson. *Courtesy Findagrave.com.*

Texas. To make the decision as to where to locate the new school, the legislature gave the responsibility to a five-member locating committee, headed by the state's populist governor, Jim "Pa" Ferguson.

Twenty-three West Texas cities and towns submitted briefs, including Lubbock, Amarillo, Snyder, Plainview, El Paso and Abilene. After visiting all twenty-three places, the five-member locating committee met in the governor's private office in Austin on June 29, 1917, to make its decision by secret ballot.

According to Lieutenant Governor William P. Hobby, a member of the committee, here is what happened: Governor Ferguson appointed a personal secretary to count the votes, but no one except the secretary saw the ballots. The secretary reported that Abilene received three of the five votes and therefore had won the coveted college. Abilene celebrated.

However, Governor Ferguson, who was known to favor Abilene, was already under suspicion of misusing funds, and the others soon questioned the vote. After the meeting, only one of the other four would admit to voting for Abilene. Two may have voted for Snyder and another for El Paso. It seemed obvious that the governor had rigged the vote.

When word of the deception spread, West Texans demanded that the locating committee meet again, but other charges against Ferguson sealed his demise. Just three weeks after the irregular vote, Ferguson was indicted on nine charges of embezzlement and misuse of funds by a Travis County grand jury, and in September 1917, he was impeached by the legislature and removed from office.

The West Texas A&M Campaign Committee thought it best to just start over and asked new governor William Hobby to repeal the bill. Hobby agreed, and the action seemingly squashed the West Texas dream of its own A&M college. However, out of the movement, the West Texas Chamber of Commerce was created in late 1918, and its sole purpose was to secure an A&M college.

That fight would require another five years, but it was an effort that would eventually lead to the creation of the Texas Technological College in 1923 and whose impartial locating committee would choose Lubbock over thirty-six competing communities.

Perhaps Lubbock should have honored the deposed Governor Ferguson, for as one prominent observer noted in the 1920s, had it not been for Ferguson's shenanigans, "the college would have stayed in Abilene…and Ferguson would not have been impeached…and hence Lubbock would have never gotten Texas Tech."

In a sense, West Texas got both Texas Tech and its long-coveted A&M. In 1922, the normal college at Canyon became known as West Texas State Teachers College and, in 1963, West Texas State University. In 1990, the state placed the school in the Texas A&M University System, and in 1992, it was renamed West Texas A&M University.

Chapter 35

Slaton and the Ku Klux Klan, 1921–1926

Robert Sledge

The Ku Klux Klan sprang up in the South during the Reconstruction era after the Civil War as a vehicle for empowering disenfranchised southern whites. Its notorious and illegal activities continued until 1877, when Reconstruction officially ended and the Klan disbanded.

Resurrected in 1915 as a fraternal organization, the second manifestation of the Klan soon took on a familiar cast. In the 1920s, the Ku Klux Klan became the vehicle for small-town Americans to protest changing cultural mores.

The "Klan of the twenties," wrote one historian, "was an enemy not only of Negroes but also of Catholics, Jews, radicals, immigrants, bootleggers, moral offenders, habitual criminals, modernist theologians, and assorted other types."

The Ku Klux Klan caught on in Slaton in the summer of 1921, at about the same time that the organization was sweeping the state. Its membership came mainly from the middle class, including professionals, merchants and public officials—often the town's movers and shakers.

The Klan strongly opposed violations that seemed beyond the reach of constituted authorities. Wife-beating, swearing, sponsorship of "immoral" motion pictures and literature, adultery and drunkenness fell into such categories. The Klan tried to stop bootlegging of alcohol but with only mixed success. About prostitution, one Klansman said, "I seen them whup the devil out of a feller there in Slaton. He was takin' a little girl out and sellin' her to them railroad men. Well...the Ku Klux took him out one night...and they breshed his hind end off with a double end rope."

Slaton's Klavern, as local groups were called, indulged in typical Klan rituals. In July 1924, for example, the group held a parade with nearly three thousand members participating. An estimated ten thousand people watched as the hooded figures bore a fiery cross and a large American flag through the streets.

Likewise, the local Klavern held "church visitations." In a typical incident, several hooded figures marched down the aisle of Slaton's First Baptist Church during Sunday services and handed the minister, Pastor John P. Hardesty, a bundle of money in appreciation of him and his church. A Klan visitation more often was an occasion for trouble, as happened to a farmer who struck his wife. The woman had come to town in the early 1920s with blackened eyes, the victim of a wife-beater. The Klan paid the husband a visit, threatened him and assured him much worse would befall him if such an event occurred again.

Perhaps the most notorious Klan-related event in Slaton was the "lynching" of a Catholic priest, Father Josef M. Keller. A German immigrant, Keller was an outspoken supporter of Germany in a strong anti-German era. Further, Keller's eccentricities made him unpopular among his congregation. The Klan and other local folks leveled several charges against him. Others accused him of sexual immorality with some of his female parishioners.

As a result, one evening in early spring 1922, a group of masked men kidnapped Father Keller and carried him off into the nighttime prairie. According to a Slaton historian, Klan members seized him at his home and hauled him off bound and gagged, wearing only his robe and house slippers. On the prairie several miles out of town, the mob stripped Keller and lashed him badly. Then, its members covered him with hot tar and feathers. The perpetrators left him to his own devices as they drove away.

Father Keller at his home in Slaton, 1922. *Courtesy James Villanueva, from his book* Remembering Slaton, Texas: Centennial Stories, 1911–2011.

Keller eventually stumbled back to town, wearing only one house slipper plus the coat of tar. He found a doctor who engaged in the long and painful process of removing the tar. Quickly afterward, Father Keller left Slaton, never to return.

Baptist minister John Hardesty wrote, "I know that Slaton was a clean town for the duration of the Klan in that community....I do know that the law enforcement officers, school trustees, many of the county officials, including the sheriff, were Klansmen, and that the backbone of the evangelical churches of the community consisted of Klansmen, and that they stood for the enforcement of law, and for clean living."

By 1926, the Ku Klux Klan was in decline, exposed not so much as a grand movement but more as a malicious national con based on membership fees and purchases of Klan paraphernalia.

Klan fervor in Slaton dissipated too, and life resumed a more familiar routine—crops, schools, business, the weather, church—typical of small-town America.

Chapter 36

The Thanksgiving Day Sandstorm, 1926

Paul H. Carlson

Thursday, November 24, 2016, marked the ninetieth anniversary of one of the most destructive sandstorms to hit the South Plains and the near Southwest. If newspaper reports are correct, some eighty people died during the 1926 storm, most in Texas and Arkansas. Very high winds with gritty dust and sand damaged crops, wrecked buildings and made Thanksgiving dinners miserable.

As the *Dallas Morning News* quaintly put it, "Lubbock [residents] ate Thanksgiving turkey Thursday generously interspersed with grit."

In the early twentieth century, but especially during World War I and afterward, farmers began plowing the High Plains in what some have come to call the "big plow up." After they turned the lush pastures into cultivated fields, farmers found that high winds picked up dry earth and carried it away. And on November 25, 1926, the combination of high winds and blowing sand created disaster over the South Plains. One person wrote, "I thought the world was coming to an end."

In Littlefield, merchant Ed Aryain called it "the worst sandstorm ever to hit West Texas." During it, he wrote, I "could not see across the street. The air was so filled with sand that it sifted into every house and business."

"Sand lay so thick across the front of my store," he wrote, "that I had to get a shovel and push the sand away."

William G. DeLoach indicated that on his farm near Sudan in Lamb County, the wind blew all day. "I thought the house would go.... [I] could not see 100 [yards] down the road."

In the Hockley County area, according to historian Bill Billingsley, the sandstorm "literally harvested that year's cotton crop." An estimated five thousand bales of cotton in the county were blown away or destroyed.

In Lamb County, 80 percent of the cotton bolls had been blown off the stalks, and according to Aryain, what "little remained was so damaged and brown and filled with sand that it was hardly worth picking and sending to market." DeLoach wrote that the "cotton…is all out and ruined."

In Levelland, the Texas Utilities Power plant building was demolished, leaving local citizens without lights and electrical power until Friday evening. Many houses lost their roofs, and others were moved from their foundations.

The "sweeping sandstorm," as the *Dallas Morning News* called it, began shortly after 4:00 a.m. on Thanksgiving Day. A gale-like wind, it came from the northwest, blew constantly at fifty miles per hour, roared through much of the near Southwest and continued until after sundown.

As noted, damage was considerable. In some towns, the wind demolished automobile tops and moved some cars from parking places into the middle of the streets. Street and store signs blew down or were permanently twisted out of shape.

In Slaton, the wind blew down an awning in the business district, striking and instantly killing J.B. Hartman. The man left behind his wife and several children.

Because the storm created a generous amount of static electricity, barbed-wire fences sparked along the roads, sometimes causing grass fires. In Dallas, people feared such grass fires, and several blazes started. The local paper reported that "fires, fanned by a gale that blew practically all day [on Thanksgiving], were responsible for 30-odd fire alarms." In Littlefield, a new cotton gin burned down.

The storm also destroyed a South Plains landmark: the 132-foot-tall windmill in *Casas Amarillas* (Yellow Houses) basin. Built by the XIT Ranch about 1887 and reportedly the tallest windmill in the world at the time, the thirty-eight-year-old wood-frame structure collapsed in the wind.

The big storm brought at least two benefits. First, when A.H. Macha, a farmer near Tahoka, surveyed his ruined cotton crop, "he discovered," according to historian Janet Neugebauer, a few plants "with the lint so tightly compacted in the burr that [they] had escaped damage." He saved the seeds and, over the next few years, replanted "the storm-proof bolls." In 1934, Macha approached agricultural officials with his results, and eventually a commercial variety of storm-proof cotton, called Macha, appeared.

Second, because cotton growers paid pickers by the pound and the storm put heavy sand into the bolls, hand picking became financially impractical. As a result, farmers began using "cotton sleds," or "slides," most of which were homemade, to skid through the fields and strip off the bolls. Mechanical strippers came soon afterward.

In such ways, perhaps, the Thanksgiving Day storm changed the face of West Texas, but as Billingsley has written, "however bad it was, the 1926 storm was only a harbinger" of what followed in the Dust Bowl days of the 1930s.

Chapter 37

The "Black Sunday" Dust Blizzard, April 14, 1935

Paul H. Carlson

Through much of the 1930s, the southern Great Plains suffered through drought and blowing dirt and dust. Many of the dust storms were severe, such as ones occurring on May 9, 1934, and March 3, 1935. But no "dust blizzard" was as dramatic as the one on Sunday, April 14, 1935. "It looked as black as tar paper, boiling over, all crumpled and wrapping around itself," said Arch Lamb, a Texas Tech freshman in 1935. "I was frightened by it."

In high-billowing dust clouds, the "Black Sunday" storm rolled south through the Llano Estacado. It moved at speeds estimated between eighty-five miles per hour in Amarillo and sixty miles per hour in Lubbock. The day got dark as night. Chickens went to roost. Automobiles stalled. Driving became dangerous. Birds flew close to the ground, attracted by lights, including those of automobiles.

Because the early afternoon was pleasant and sunny, many people were outside when the dust blizzard hit. Lubbock resident Weston Petty said, "I never saw anything like it. The day got dark as night."

At least one group was playing golf that Sunday. "We saw it coming," said Cliff Edwards. "We thought it was rain. By the time it got close enough for us to see the rolling dust we were in its very middle. We could see nothing—there was absolute blackness."

The storm's front hit hard. Petty said that after the front edge hit an area, conditions outside were "completely black for fifteen minutes, but the dark dust stayed around until nightfall."

The "Black Sunday" dust storm hit Spearman in the upper Panhandle around noon on April 14, 1935. *National Archives.*

Dust penetrated supposedly airtight buildings and, once inside, permeated everything. Dirt collected in corners and settled thickly on floor rugs. In Lubbock apparel shops, exposed surfaces of colorful clothes gathered enough dust to appear as only varying shades of gray and brown. New shoes on display lost their bright luster and gathered dust.

In homes, adults watched over infant children. A woman in Lockney reported that mothers with babies "put them to sleep and spread a blanket" or sheet over the crib. Many women put wet cloths across the mouths and over the faces of their sleeping children.

On roads and highways of the South Plains, motorists switched on automobile headlights. When visibility "became zero or lower," as one newspaper editor put it, drivers "pulled off the roads and stopped their cars" or drove into the ditches to wait out the black blizzard.

Raleigh Middleton said the storm "was miserable for animals." He indicated they became "covered solid with dust and couldn't breathe." Viola Lowry indicated that "any animals that were out in [the blizzard]...their noses, their faces and eyes would be just covered in dirt."

The black blizzard left Lubbock's spring grass with a gray coating. Lamb indicated that as he walked across the Tech campus on Monday morning, little puffs of powdery dust rose with each step he took.

A more distressing result of Black Sunday was dust pneumonia. Frank Hill and Pat Jacobs in Lynn County wrote that nearly everyone "exposed to the storm found his nose, throat, and lungs filled with dust." Joe Christian, who lived near Seagraves, said "dust pneumonia like to got me."

In Ralls, a Baptist preacher climbed to the top of a building to watch the approaching storm. "He took dust pneumonia," reported a local resident. In Ralls, another person wrote with too much hyperbole, "there was at least a funeral a day, of those who had contacted [*sic*] pneumonia from the dust."

After the dramatic front had passed, dust and silt settled to a depth of "an eighth of an inch, possibly more." The silt contained nitrates, phosphoric acid and potash. A government analysis of the silt reported that it "was far richer in plant food value than much of the local soil." An eighth of an inch of the silt, said a Tech professor, was worth per acre "about five to fifteen wagon loads of barnyard fertilizer."

Perhaps the most unique aspect of the Black Sunday storm was the high amount of static electricity it contained. The static electricity caused lights to blink and electrical power to falter.

Finally, the term "Dust Bowl" came from Black Sunday. Associated Press reporter Robert Geiger in a newspaper dispatch began his story, "Three little words achingly familiar on a Western farmer's tongue, rule life in the dust bowl of the continent—if it rains."

The *Lubbock Evening Journal* and other newspapers carried the dispatch the next day. Since then, "Dust Bowl" has defined the 1930s drought.

Chapter 38

The Lubbock Flood, May 20, 1941

Paul H. Carlson

May 1941 was a wet month. "In only three days this month," reported the *Lubbock Morning Journal* on May 4, there "has been nearly as much rain as the whole of May for any year in the past 30 years."

It kept falling—not only in Lubbock and the South Plains but also across the state. Also on May 4, the paper stated, "According to most competent estimate more than [300 million] gallons" of water are headed down Yellow House Draw "through Buffalo Lake to the Gulf of Mexico."

On May 6, the paper reported highways closed in the Austin area. It noted that the "North Fork of the Red [River] in Oklahoma was rising one foot per hour. The river was a mile wide west of Terrell bridge."

The rain encouraged all manner of flora to bloom. "Get out and see wild flowers—rain has blessed the area with wild flowers not seen in years," editors of the *Morning Journal* suggested. And a headline on May 5 read: "South Plains Has Sufficient Moisture to Carry Crops through Until August."

As the rain continued, people sought umbrellas, raincoats and overshoes. "I could have sold a carload of overcoats," one merchant said. Another indicated he even "could have sold hip boots if I had them."

The rain in early to mid-May, according to the Lubbock paper, became "one of the longest raining spells on record." Few days were without moisture. A tornado swept through northern Lubbock County on May 10 and then with fury struck Hale County before moving southeastward into Crosby County. Three people died: a couple in Hale County when their home was hit and a man in Crosby County struck by lightning.

On the thirteenth of the month, the Lubbock paper reported "increasing chances of rain Tuesday and Wednesday with scattered showers developing in the afternoon."

Then, on May 20, according to the *Morning Journal*, Lubbock suffered "one of the hardest rains here in 15 years." On the twenty-first, the paper noted that "precipitation of near-cloudburst proportions fell in the city during the morning closing to traffic underpasses on both east [East Broadway] and north [old Amarillo Highway] entrances to town."

"The downpour came suddenly," the paper reported, "and was accompanied by small hail." Motor vehicles "stalled throughout the city." In the East Broadway underpass, two automobiles "were completely covered with water and a light truck nearly was submerged."

Through much of the city, "water flowed over curbs...and several business houses were partially flooded." Some $15,000 in damage occurred "to paper stock at Carpenter Paper Company."

Several people took to small boats and, using oars, navigated the downtown streets.

The rain was no less damaging in rural areas of Lubbock County. Wheat fields were covered with water. New Deal school officials did not send the children home on buses but arranged to have them boarded in community homes until parents could get to town.

At several farms, livestock suffered from too much water. On the L.C. Boyd farm northeast of Lubbock, unfortunately, thirty hogs and pigs and 130 chickens drowned.

Water ran over the curb in downtown Lubbock in May 1941, allowing for boat transportation. *Courtesy Southwest Collection, Texas Tech University.*

Despite the scattered livestock damage, officials reported that "the flash shower [on May 20] was primarily confined to Lubbock." Rain poured down in the morning, and not until about three o'clock in the afternoon did traffic activity begin to return to normal. The blocked underpasses became usable again about five o'clock.

Several inches of rain fell that morning. Flooding ensued in part because the ground in both Lubbock and the county was saturated. Nearly 16.00 inches of rain had fallen since January 1, and of that amount, about 8.87 inches of rain came down between May 1 and May 20, when the flooding occurred.

A few additional inches of rain came down during the last ten days of May, but no more flooding appeared. A total of 12.69 inches fell during the month, more rain than occurred for the entire year of 2015, when Lubbock recorded only 12.12 inches of moisture.

Since 1911, when officials began keeping such records, the wettest month in Lubbock has been, surprisingly, September 1936, near the end of the long drought of the Dust Bowl years, when officials recorded 13.93 inches of rainfall.

The year 1941 ranks as the wettest on record, with a total of 40.55 inches of rain. In fact, no other year is close to that total. In 1915, officials listed a total of 31.88 inches of rain—the nearest challenger.

Still, the May 20, 1941 rainfall, while not the city's largest single rain event, closed Lubbock streets, shut down traffic, flooded several businesses, brought boats to the downtown area and filled Yellow House Draw above Buffalo Springs to near its very limits.

Chapter 39

The Lubbock Tornado, May 11, 1970

Paul H. Carlson

The huge tornado that brought Lubbock temporarily to its knees struck the city about 9:46 p.m. on May 11, 1970. An F5-category storm, it was a powerful, swirling tempest with high winds, hail and heavy rainfall.

The massive storm caught Lubbock and its citizens by surprise. The day had been warm and humid, and there was little indication of a major weather event. But early that Monday evening, winds picked up, clouds moved in and a bit of rain fell. About dusk, some accounts note, a spinning, high wind struck near Sixty-Sixth Street and University Avenue, leaving, before it dissipated, plenty of property damage.

There may have been one or two other twisters involved. But a bit later, most reports suggest, a powerful, churning tornado with very high winds, hail and heavy rainfall dropped out of the dark night sky near Nineteenth Street and University.

The giant storm cut a wide swath. As it circled its way through the heart of the city with winds that may have reached well over two hundred miles per hour, it moved toward and into the downtown area. Then, suddenly, it turned to the north to smash with massive destructiveness through the neighborhood north of Thirteenth Street and the Guadalupe community beyond Fourth Street.

If in fact it was a single tornado, it continued toward the north along the Amarillo Highway (Highway 87, now I-27) and, before dissipating shortly after ten o'clock, leveled homes in the Country Club addition and shattered businesses along the highway. Many airplanes and small hangars

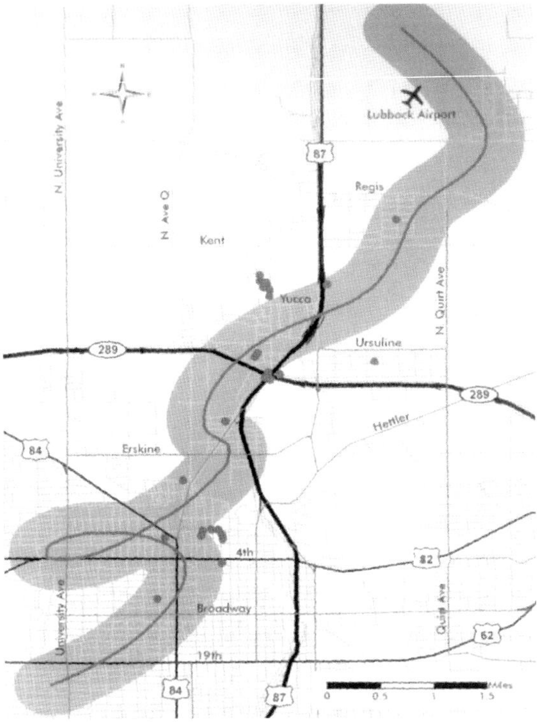

Lubbock's 1970 twister took an erratic path through the heart of the city. *Courtesy Southwest Collection, Texas Tech University.*

near the airport—West Texas Air Terminal—turned into twisted piles of their former selves.

Personal injuries and loss of life were high: 26 people died in the tornado, or tornadoes, and nearly 1,800 people suffered wounds of various kinds—255 of them seriously. The hospitals filled with scores of injured folks.

Property loss was likewise huge. The storm damaged some 10,000 homes, completely destroying 1,100 of them, many in the Guadalupe neighborhood—predominantly Mexican-American citizens. Across the tornado's curling path, perhaps 1,800 people became homeless.

Mike Cox estimated property damage totaled $840 million, making the big storm one of the costliest tornadoes in America to that time. Ten thousand automobiles sustained damage, and about five hundred businesses suffered wreckage, with some, such as the Fields & Company showroom on Fourth Street, obliterated.

The tornado was massively disruptive. Lives were lost, homes destroyed, businesses closed and jobs gone. Household goods and personal possessions disappeared. The storm scattered such small pets as cats, dogs and birds. It cut utilities, including water supplies, and it created havoc with traffic flow and communication systems. In those days before cellphones, twenty-five thousand telephones lost service. It toppled power lines and spread debris across streets, including main thoroughfares. Some underpasses filled with water, blocking access to portions of the city.

Damage to buildings, apartment houses, homes and storage facilities was widespread. Destruction extended along Fourth Street from Indiana Avenue eastward nearly to Mackenzie Park. Downtown, such structures as the stately Great Plains Life tower (present Metro Tower), the old Pioneer Hotel and the beautiful First National Bank–Pioneer Gas Building sustained heavy physical losses.

Lubbock officials immediately went to work. Mayor James Granberry announced a state of emergency and, as early as 10:00 p.m., called on the people of Lubbock to provide assistance for those in need of help.

William Payne, who headed the Emergency Operations Plan, set up a control center in the basement of city hall. Relief centers opened. KFYO, the emergency radio station, broadcast instructions, and police and National Guard troops patrolled the hardest-hit areas.

Within days, City Manager Bill Blackwell and other officials sought state and federal relief funds for projects of all kinds. In August, city voters passed a $13.6 million Disaster Recovery Bond Package.

Over time, the area along and east of Avenue Q between Fourth Street and Broadway became an urban renewal project. With bond money and federal and state funding, city leaders turned the former residential area into an entertainment, convention and business center. Motels opened along Avenue Q, and the Memorial Civic Center Complex went up.

Nearby, the city built the George and Helen Mahon Library. Texas Tech University, led by retired professor of history William Curry Holden, used debris from the destroyed homes and businesses near downtown to build a series of berms at its outdoor museum—what became the National Ranching Heritage Center.

In some ways, the 1970 tornado represents a turning point for Lubbock. The influx of federal and state money, the revitalization of the area just north and east of downtown and the dispersal of minority citizens through the city represent important and permanent transformations.

Chapter 40

The Rise and Fall of Three Way Independent School District

Jack Becker

A cement slab is all that remains of the once proud little Three Way School, located on the Llano Estacado just east of the New Mexico line in south-central Bailey County. Three Way School was located about thirty-two miles south of Muleshoe and seventy miles west of Lubbock.

Its unusual name came from the fact that in 1945, three independent school districts, Goodland, Watson and Wilson, combined into one. A year later, Three Way consolidated with Stegall School District and in 1975 with Bula School District.

Another distinguishing feature of Three Way School was its location. Situated on twenty acres of donated land, it was not within the city limits of any town. The school sat in a field surrounded by thousands of acres of cotton. In fact, there was no town of any size in the district, although the isolated village of Maple stood about 1 mile southeast of the school. At one time, the school district covered an area of 352 square miles.

For one year after consolidation in 1945, children in grades one through four went to Watson School for classes. The school building in Maple, the Wilson School, was moved to the Three Way site, and children in grades five through eight attended class there. High school students went to Goodland School.

During 1945, the first year of the new district, 349 students attended classes at the three campuses. Early in 1946, the school board voted funds to build a structure so that all the district's children could attend the same school. The new building cost $89,500 to construct.

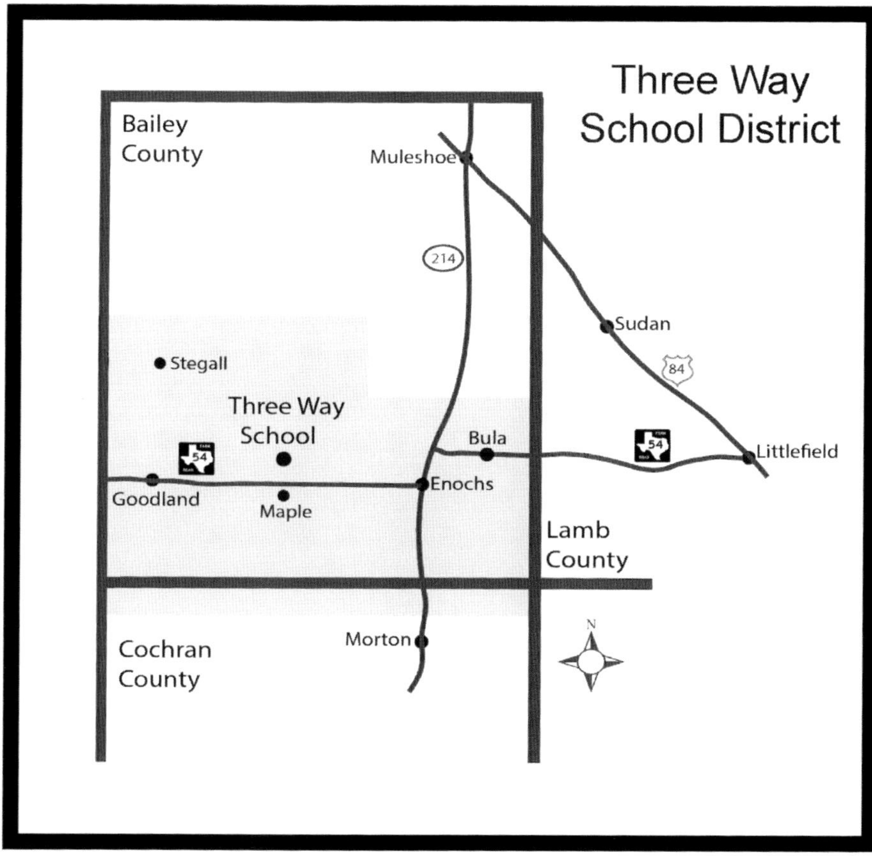

The Three Way Independent School District spread across the southern half of Bailey County and the northern edge of Cochran County, north and west of Morton. *Courtesy Curtis Peoples.*

As the years passed after consolidation, Three Way Independent School District grew, as Bailey County's population increased and new school districts joined Three Way. In 1965, the school expanded when a new library and English and business classrooms were added to the existing school. In 1974, the school expanded again, with the addition of a new home economics complex, administration offices and a kindergarten classroom. It fielded six-man football and boys' and girls' basketball teams.

Unfortunately, students of Three Way School did not enjoy their new facilities for long. In May 1977, a tornado destroyed the vocational/agricultural shop building, the football field and three teachers' apartments across the street from the school.

To help attract and keep qualified teachers in the isolated school, Three Way furnished housing for teachers. The number of faculty fluctuated along with the students but peaked at eighteen in 1977. Consistently, half of all faculty members lived on school grounds in housing provided by the school district.

In most large, rural school districts, such as Three Way, many students spent long hours riding a bus to and from school each day. Some students rode the bus more than fourteen miles one way, but they learned to make good use of their time. One student remembered spending her time on the bus reading class assignments and doing math problems—basically anything that did not require "good penmanship," for the bumpy roads did not allow that.

During its early years of existence in the 1940s and 1950s, the Three Way student population increased as the population of the counties it served grew and new school districts combined with Three Way. After the mid-1970s, school enrollment steadily dropped until only eighty-three children attended the school in 2002.

Interested citizens and the school board struggled to keep the school open, but declining enrollment and lack of adequate state funding doomed the school. When enrollment dropped below ninety students, state funding all but dried up.

In 2002, the school graduated its last senior class—one girl and six boys. The event ended over fifty years of educating southern Bailey County and northern Cochran County children. Changes in agriculture, rural economics and paved roads slowly drained population away from the Three Way School District.

In a way, its school population mirrored a decline in Bailey County's population. After years of often significant growth, the population of Bailey County peaked in 1960 at 9,090. Afterward, the population steadily dropped. In 2000, the population stood at only 6,594, with more than two-thirds (4,530) living in Muleshoe.

When it became evident the Three Way Independent School District would have to close, the people of the district voted to consolidate with the Sudan schools.

For a while, the Three Way School building remained open as a museum, dedicated to the school and the students who attended there. That building is now gone, too, and nothing more than concrete slabs indicate the school's former existence.

PART VI

LANDMARK PLACES AND EVENTS

From the ancient *Casas Amarillas* basin in Hockley County to the city of Lubbock in the 1950s, this chapter examines several major but oftentimes brief places and events of the Llano Estacado's past.

Virginia City, Ragtown and Texas Tech's inaugural football season in 1925 were short-lived, although each proved significant in the larger South Plains history. Likewise, Lubbock's World War II air training bases lasted briefly, but they, too, were major influences on the war and on life in Lubbock. Clent Breedlove's Lubbock airport also had long-range significance for air flight in general and for economic development in the city.

Until the 1950s, the remarkable Flats neighborhood, located north of Nineteenth Street and west of Avenue A in Lubbock, provided a home for a majority of the city's African American population. Another place, a little-known small rise near Lubbock known as Causey Hill, provided an observation post for bison hunters in the 1870s. These often-shrouded landmarks remain central to the area's history.

Chapter 41

Casas Amarillas

Paul H. Carlson

Casas Amarillas (Yellow Houses) are located in northern Hockley County, a short distance southwest of Littlefield. The once brown, yellowish bluffs are situated on the west side (facing east) of a wide, eight-mile, north–south oriented basin in the generally level Llano Estacado landscape. About 150 years ago, when seen at a distance from the east and especially if a mirage was present, they looked like a series of houses—hence the name.

The bluffs were pitted with shallow caves, and a spring at the base of the bluffs provided water. Two or three lakes and other water sources, including playas, could also be found in the basin.

The large, prominent depression, which at some time in the past may have drained into Yellow House Draw, gives the little valley its name. In fact, some maps show the draw cutting through the extreme southern end of the low valley.

The combination of lakes, freshwater springs and bluffs with their caves attracted early visitors to *Casas Amarillas*.

Wildlife, especially bison, deer, pronghorns, wolves and coyotes, stopped at the water holes. Native Americans used the area for hunting and camping, sometimes spending the winter there. Traders from New Mexico villages used the basin to exchange their village wears for Indian products with Comanches, Kiowas, Lipans, Mescalaros and others who frequented the popular landmark.

Bison-hide hunters, such as brothers John and George Causey, and U.S. troopers, including the Tenth Cavalry (Buffalo Soldiers), used the site. Later,

Large caves like this one on the yellow bluff prompted Spanish explorers to name it the Yellow Houses, or *Casas Amarillias*. *Courtesy Monte Monroe.*

such ranches as the XIT, George W. Littlefield's LFD and the Yellow House located their headquarters in the basin.

In the early twentieth century, *Casas Amarillas* was home to the tallest wood-frame windmill in the world, for the towering structure needed to reach from the basin floor to above the caprock high enough to catch the Llano's winds.

Several early visitors to the basin described *Casas Amarillas*. A Tenth Cavalry officer, Theodore Baldwin, said in 1875 that its walls gave "the appearance of…rocks of a yellow color."

Bison hunter turned author John Cook remembered the place in 1877 as a "bold rugged bluff with a natural and excavated cavern dug" at the base, and on the top of the bluff, above the Llano Estacado's caprock, was "a stone half-circle breastwork"; he thought Indians or comancheros had constructed the little fort.

Englishman turned bison hunter Frank Collinson wrote, "Yellow House proper was a large, yellow sandstone cave under the [caprock], opening to the east, with sufficient room for twenty or more people to camp at a time."

In 1875, Colonel William R. Shafter, while leading a military and exploring expedition across the Llano Estacado, noted, "A large alkali and salt lake, of from one-half to three-quarters of a mile in width and about three in length…[drained] the country for several miles in all directions."

Shafter reported that "there are two dug springs at the base of the bluff on the southern side, and about a half mile further south, at the head of a ravine, a large tank of fresh water" was present. He believed the springs—later called, appropriately enough, Yellow House Springs—fed the lake. After camping at the site for a couple of days and using the springs for both horses and men, Shafter still found plenty of water available.

Two years later, *Casas Amarillas* played a prominent role in a joint bison hunter–Buffalo Soldier effort to find a small party of Comanches who had not gone to their reservation in Indian Territory (Oklahoma). The hunters and soldiers lost their way during the July 1877 operation, ran out of water and resorted to drinking their own and their horses' urine. Four soldiers died. But a few soldiers and several hunters who had drifted away from the main force found their way to the refreshing water in *Casas Amarillas*. As soon as they had recovered, they sought to bring water to their suffering companions.

Today, *Casas Amarillas* is on private property, land belonging to the Yellow House Ranch. Although the primary site is not available to the public, the southern edge of the basin can be seen from the Hockley County road that passes by the ranch entrance. And *Casas Amarillas*, its east-facing bluffs green with grass and weeds, remains a dramatic view.

Chapter 42

Lubbock County's Causey Hill

Robert L. Carr and Paul H. Carlson

Causey Hill is named for bison hunters John V. and Thomas L. "George" Causey. Located in Lubbock County between Lubbock and Idalou, the hill rises only about fifty feet above the surrounding countryside, but in the nineteenth century, it was an important landmark for humans in the area.

Situated a few miles beyond the limits of the city of Lubbock on property of the local Texas Boys Ranch north of U.S. Highways 62 and 82 and State Highway 114, it is barely noticeable by someone racing past in an automobile. Yet Causey Hill has a storied history, one that dates to at least the coming of bison hunters to the region in the 1870s. In 1874, bison-hide hunters and bison-hide buyers entered the Texas Panhandle to hunt the large brown animals, for bison hides were in high demand in eastern cities. Hunter camps appeared along many creeks.

Several hunters, hide buyers, traders and others established a short-lived trading post they called Adobe Walls. Located near the site of an old trading post along the Canadian River in the upper Texas Panhandle, it contained mud and sod buildings and a wagon road that connected it to Dodge City, the busy cattle and hide town in Kansas.

Angry about the hunter camps and the Adobe Walls trading post, Indian warriors, including Comanche and Cheyenne, attacked the trading post in 1874, but they soon withdrew. In response, the U.S. Army in August sent some three thousand soldiers into the Panhandle to find the Indians and return them to their reservations. The fighting that followed became known as the Red River War. It did not go well for the Indians, and by late

November, most of the warriors had returned to their reservations with their families.

After the war, in early 1875, hunters with skinners and teamsters renewed their assault on Panhandle and Southern Plains bison herds. Camps and trading posts spread across a huge area of West Texas, extending southward to the Concho River country.

Among the hunting camps were those of the Causey brothers. In 1877, the Causeys set up a camp at Buffalo Springs in Yellow House Canyon just below present-day Lubbock.

It was a typical bison hunting camp. Hides, for example, lay pegged out on the ground over a wide area, bison tongues hung to sun-dry on racks, tents stood nearby and a wagon or two waited to be loaded with hides for hauling to market at short-lived Rath City in Stonewall County or Fort Griffin farther east in Shackelford County.

From their camp in the canyon, George Causey on most days rode out to the slight rise, Causey Hill, to sight bison herds. The hill was about eleven miles north of his camp, and once at the top of the little knoll, or so the story goes, Causey stood up erect in the saddle on his horse. Then, using his binoculars, he viewed the flat land reaching away toward the horizon as he looked for herds that he would hunt for the day.

George Causey was one of the most successful—or destructive—bison hunters who operated on the Great Plains. Over time, he killed far more bison, for example, than the famed Buffalo Bill Cody, and during the 1877–78 hunting season alone, Causey slaughtered thousands of animals.

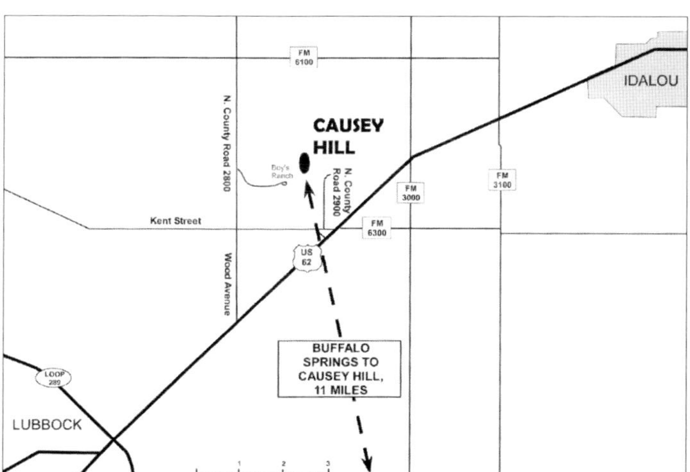

Causey Hill is located to the north of the Texas Boys Ranch in northeastern Lubbock County. *Map by David J. Murrah.*

Although it is Lubbock County's most prominent upland, Causey Hill is not the county's highest elevation. It crests out at approximately 3,225 feet. But because, like much of the Llano Estacado, the county's land surface tends to higher elevations toward the north and west, the highest point in Lubbock County reaches to 3,300 feet. Still, land surrounding Causey Hill is essentially flat, and one's view in the nineteenth century was limited only by the horizon.

The Causeys did not stay long at their Buffalo Springs camp. They soon moved up the canyon to *Casas Amarillas*, the large basin about forty miles west of Lubbock. Eventually, George Causey moved to New Mexico.

Nonetheless, the name for the slight rise that was important to the Causey hunting operation at Buffalo Springs has stuck. Today, Causey Hill, about nine miles northeast of downtown Lubbock, can be seen as a gentle rise before one approaches the tiny community of Kitalou, but it is much more accentuated if approached and viewed from county roads on its west side.

Today, people at the Texas Boys Ranch raise wheat and graze cattle on the inconspicuous little round mound that played a brief but historic role in the bison hunting exploits of John and George Causey.

Chapter 43

Virginia City in Bailey County, Texas

Dolores Mosser

Virginia City in Bailey County, Texas, rose and fell over a four-year period between 1909 and 1913, doomed by drought and rural isolation. The town was the dream of Matthew C. Vaughn, an enterprising young man from Waterloo, Iowa. He wanted to build the town in the heart of Bailey County. His idea was to sell cheap land to midwesterners wanting to escape worn soils and seeking to make new lives.

Vaughn and his partner, Samuel D. McCloud, platted the town and located it in central Bailey County in 1908. It overlooked Monument Lake and stood near a historic road that crossed the Llano Estacado from its eastern caprock westward to the Pecos River. The town plat showed 166 city blocks with residential and commercial lots. Vaughn and McCloud reserved city blocks for parks, schools, a library and the hoped-for Bailey County Courthouse. They laid out streets, alleys and a lakeshore drive and moved a two-story hotel, the Virginia City Hotel, onto the town site to accommodate guests and prospective area settlers and townspeople.

They oversaw the construction of grading for a railway track for what they called the Denver and San Antonio Railroad. Vaughn and McCloud believed in late 1908 that prospective land seekers on inspection tours would soon arrive by railroad at Muleshoe. From there, the future citizens would travel overland the twenty-five miles southwest to Virginia City, which "opened for business" in 1909.

Matthew Vaughn was a "land speculator," a businessman, who, like C.W. Post, W.P. Soash and others, looked out across the wide-open prairies of the

Llano Estacado and envisioned small farms, anchored by towns with homes, businesses, schools and churches.

Vaughn and his partner, through their M.C. Vaughn Land Company, meant to replicate the successes of Post and Soash, who also was from Waterloo, Iowa. According to *The Handbook of Texas*, "In 1905 [Soash] founded the W.P. Soash Land Company, which grew to be one of the largest land companies in the United States, with offices in more than eight states." Soash bought and sold XIT and C.C. Slaughter ranch lands with land promotion tactics that appealed to Vaughn and McCloud.

To accommodate land-seekers, speculators like Vaughn and Soash built hotels and other structures in such western Llano Estacado towns as Bovina, Farwell, Friona, Whiteface and Virginia City. Railroad tours brought prospective farmers into the plains, where they inspected the unbroken soils and selected farm sites. The trains often traveled at night to remove any fear the new arrivals might have of the Llano's wide-open spaces.

Matthew Vaughn advertised his lands with glowing reports of the plentiful rains and bountiful crops. He noted that water, an important marketing tool, was in abundance from high levels of ground water in the underlying Ogallala Aquifer. Iowa newspapers praised the land that Vaughn and McCloud made available through their company, and promotional photographs showed beautiful crops growing in the area. Advertisements also illustrated harvest fair exhibits of garden vegetables, alfalfa, corn, wheat, sorghum, peanuts and apples and attributed the prized harvests to perfect soils, good weather and plenty of water.

With ease of shipping, plenty of water, good soils and scenic terrain, Virginia City, Vaughn argued, would be the perfect prairie community.

Twice a month in automobiles, Vaughn's company employees drove prospective buyers from Portales, New Mexico, to Virginia City to see the grasslands, sand hills and salt lakes of central Bailey County.

In a related promotional campaign, L.W. Fiscus, a Vaughn associate, arranged an automobile excursion from Portales to Lubbock to witness the Santa Fe Railroad's arrival in the Hub City. Participants began the trip on October 28, 1909, with stops at Vaughn's Virginia City Hotel and later the Yellow House Ranch, owned by another land promoter, George W. Littlefield. In Lubbock, the Fiscus excursion group helped to celebrate the first train, with thirty-five passengers, leaving the Santa Fe Railroad depot. The adventure lasted three days, covered 195 miles and, as reported by a Portales newspaper, was completed "without a mishap or breakdown and not a thing done to the cars except oil and replenish the gas."

The state historical marker stands in Bailey County where Virginia City grew and declined in the early 1900s. *Courtesy Paul H. Carlson.*

Virginia City's story was not as successful. Similar to the story of the town of Soash in Howard County, three years of severe drought brought Vaughn's "Dream City" to an end. People left their farms and abandoned the town. Vaughn sold the Virginia City Hotel to Maple Wilson, who moved it to his farm. Years later, Mrs. Wilson forgot that the old structure was once a hotel. The restored building is now located at the Muleshoe Heritage Center.

The Denver and San Antonio Railroad was little more than part of Vaughn's scheme for his town. A charter for the railroad was neither requested nor secured, but a survey map shows a railroad route running south from Muleshoe.

All that remains of Virginia City's former presence is a short railroad grade along Highway 1731, twenty-five miles southwest of Muleshoe, and a Texas historical marker pointing to the location of Matthew Vaughn's "dream city."

This essay is from a forthcoming larger study of the Portales Valley Trail of Living Waters.

Chapter 44

C.W. Post's "Ragtown" in Garza County, Texas

J'Nell Pate Barnes

How does a community get the name "Ragtown"? Someone I knew before she passed away at age eighty-five told family and friends that her mother and her family came to West Texas in the early part of the twentieth century to a place they called "Ragtown."

As two of us drove through Post, Texas, not long ago, we saw a sign reading, "Ragtown Gospel Theatre." We decided to find out about Ragtown.

In the city of Post, we found an incredible museum in a two-story, rock former sanitarium (hospital), and the museum director, Linda Puckett, told us how to drive to what is left of Ragtown. We drove there to find an old, empty two-story school and a few houses of people still living in the area. The school was built in 1919 and replaced an earlier wooden building.

Actually, the official name of the town was Close City, named after Marjorie Merriweather Post Close, who had married Edward Close but divorced him after having two daughters. Marjorie's father, C.W. Post, the wealthy cereal maker (Post Toasties and others), had purchased over 330,000 acres (515 sections) in the Garza County area. He planned a town to be located on the high bluff above the caprock, and there he laid out Close City.

He later discovered that state law required a county seat town to be near the middle of the county. Thus, he moved east and down off the Llano Estacado to a lower elevation where his new town site would comply with Texas law. At the new site, Post sought to build a "planned community." He called it Post City. He built a rock home in the town and used his considerable fortune to construct public buildings, churches, a hospital and

The former Close City school is located in what was known as Ragtown at the turn of the century. *Courtesy Paul H. Carlson.*

other buildings. He also divided his huge landholdings into 160-acre farms to sell with a small down payment and a twenty-year payoff. He wanted to assist farmers in owning their own land.

At the point in each section where the four 160-acre farms met, Post dug a well. He built a house in each of the four meeting corners so that families living there would be neighbors. Within two years, he had built seven hundred houses.

Meanwhile, folks who first settled in Close City or on surrounding farms lived mainly in tents, intending, of course, to build more permanent homes. While living in their tents on that high bluff, the wind blew with great force. Being buffeted almost constantly by strong winds, the tents couldn't withstand the strain and became torn and ragged. Thus, the early settlers called their little community up on the caprock "Ragtown."

Mrs. T.E. Fortune was one of them. She said her husband and older sons preceded her to the area, but she arrived with the youngest child, a daughter, in 1915. Her husband had purchased 160 acres three miles west of Close City.

"I was the proudest human to own that farm," she said. "It was the first farm we ever owned." She said they traded in Ragtown at a general store that took care of most of their immediate needs. They called Charlie Everett, who ran the store, "Ragtown Charlie." She said that the land was fertile, and "we never came to town without something to sell."

Ragtown sounds like a typical frontier town, but it did not grow as its neighbor Post City did after it secured a railroad in 1910. C.W. Post died on May 9, 1914, of a self-inflicted gunshot wound before he could see how his town became prosperous.

Post's daughter Marjorie, after her divorce, married E.F. Hutton, a financier, and they had one daughter who later became the actress Dina Merrill.

Marjorie Merriweather Post Close Hutton, because of her father's cereal fortune and her husband's great capital, became "the wealthiest woman in the United States." She owned a fabulous estate in Florida called Mar-a-Lago, but later sold it. Its owner in 2017 was Donald Trump.

Because of hundreds of producing oil wells in the area, many millionaires live in Post or elsewhere in Garza County. None of them live in Ragtown.

Chapter 45

Texas Tech's Inaugural Football Season, 1925

David J. Murrah

At long last, in 1925, college football finally made it to Lubbock. On October 3 of that year, Texas Tech's Matadors kicked off the first-ever college game in Lubbock against the McMurry College Indians from Abilene.

It wasn't the first college game on the South Plains; that honor went to Clarendon College when it defeated the nearby Goodnight Academy 16–10 on December 5, 1903. However, the schools were only junior colleges.

Senior college football came a little later. By 1925, nearby West Texas State College at Canyon had been playing football for fifteen years, although most of its opponents had been high school teams or the scattered little church junior colleges—Goodnight Baptist College at Goodnight, Wayland Baptist and Seth Ward at Plainview, Hereford Christian at Hereford and Simmons College in Abilene. WT's first game in 1910 was a 36–0 victory over Amarillo High School.

As soon as Texas Tech was created and Lubbock announced as its location, the school's fielding a football team was one of the community's highest priorities. Long before the college opened, Lubbock supporters had formed a booster club, now the Red Raider Club. It wanted big-time football. However, for its inaugural season, Tech had to schedule anyone who would play, and the college chose opponents who were closest to Lubbock.

Little McMurry College was beginning its third season of football. Its 1924 team went 4-1, its only loss to Sul Ross State. And McMurry had a head start on the 1925 season. The Indians had already played two games before

The first Texas Tech football game ever, against McMurry in 1925 at the Lubbock fairgrounds. *From* The Totem: McMurry College Year Book, 1924, *Portal to Texas History (online), University of North Texas Libraries.*

playing Tech, going 1-1 against Daniel Baker College from Brownwood and Meridian Junior College. Tech's Matadors, however, had only practiced for two weeks. A total of 137 players had showed up for Tech's first workout.

Nonetheless, the Tech-McMurry game was big-time college football for the five thousand or more fans attending the game at the South Plains Fair Grounds. Agriculture professor W.L. Stangel led a crew of students trying to sweep goat head stickers from the field. On the opposite side, a tall, lanky McMurry teacher cheering on his team caught the eye of a Lubbock newspaper reporter.

"W.C. Holden, head of the History Department at McMurry College, is not a football star, but is effective on the sideline and knows every member of the Indian aggregation by name," the *Lubbock Avalanche* noted, and "members of that team will readily confess that he was right in there from the start and carried a big part of the Load."

Within four years, Holden would be teaching at Tech, and both he and Stangel would have major impacts on the school. Today, two buildings on the campus bear their names: Holden Hall and Stangel Hall.

The opening game was nothing like the air-raid offense played by Tech today. Neither team had scored as time was running out. Tech kicked a twenty-yard field goal, but the referee ruled that time had expired just before the kick. Thus, Tech's football history began with a scoreless tie.

The team made up for its lack of offense later in the season. Tech defeated Wayland Baptist 120–0, its highest point total ever. Even today's air-raid offenses will probably not exceed that total.

There were other memorable highlights in 1925. Tech scored its first points, a field goal, in a 3–3 tie with Austin College and made its first touchdown against Montezuma College in its first ever win, 30–0. In its first games against traditional West Texas football powers, Tech beat Sul Ross State in Alpine 21–7 but then lost to Howard Payne College in Brownwood, 30–0. Thus, it finished the season at a respectable 6-1-2, especially after winning its long-anticipated game with West Texas State, 13–12.

Embedded in that first season were the hopes of future success. In Tech's second game in 1925, the 3–3 tie with Austin College, Lubbock's fans were introduced to Pete Cawthon, the twenty-seven-year-old fiery young coach of the Kangaroos. Five years later, Cawthon became Tech's third head coach, and during his eleven-year tenure from 1930 to 1940, his teams went 78-32-6, winning more games than any other Tech coach.

During that time, the Matadors became the nationally known Red Raiders, the highest-scoring team in the country. They made back-to-back bowl games (Sun and Cotton) in 1937 and 1938, going undefeated during the 1938 regular season, the only team in Tech's history to do so. And it all began in that banner year of 1925.

Chapter 46

Lubbock's "The Flats" Neighborhood

Paul H. Carlson

The Flats" neighborhood in Lubbock extended from Avenue A to Avenue C between Sixteenth and Nineteenth Streets. Except in memory, it no longer exists as a subdivision, but the small, dynamic area was home in the 1920s and afterward to many of the city's African American residents. As the community's black population increased, many of its citizens moved to newer residential additions, such as Carver Heights (Chatman Hill) or Manhattan Heights, in east Lubbock.

After an urban renewal and redevelopment movement in the 1960s, The Flats as an active neighborhood ceased to exist. From its heyday, only a church building, now St. Paul Historic Church, and the former Caviel Drug Store at 1719 Avenue A remain. The drugstore building has become a museum for the Lubbock Roots Historical Arts Council.

Before 1960, The Flats was a cohesive community with homes, many businesses, schools, churches, a Masonic lodge and, according to historian Katie Parks, "various nefarious activities." Such activities included bootlegging of alcoholic beverages during the national Prohibition years of the 1920s and afterward.

The little community attracted many of the first black Americans arriving in Lubbock. Although the date of the first arrivals is unknown, in 1910, a local newspaper warned black Americans to stay clear of the city. In early 1917, city council minutes listed sixteen African Americans in Lubbock.

Ben Shields and Calvin Quigley, who operated a rooming house on Avenue A, sheltered many of the first arrivals. The people stayed until cotton growers hired them to pull bolls. After the cotton harvest, many pickers drifted back into town.

Some of them, according to Katie Parks, took positions as maids, cooks or servants at homes west of downtown, a place The Flats' residents called "Out on the Hill." Myrtle Williams and her sister Ola Mae West cooked for over forty years for a family that lived on Seventeenth Street "Out on the Hill." For a time, Ola Mae, Myrtle and her husband, Charles C. Williams, operated a grocery store in their home. Williams also worked as a barber. In addition, writes Parks, he "traveled all over the West Texas area at night, playing for dances" and becoming known as "Drum-beating Charlie."

With the tract surrounded by cotton-oil mills, warehouses, a cotton compress and railroad tracks, many residents found jobs nearby. They bought lots in the subdivision and built homes, sometimes using scrap lumber, tin and other scavenged materials. In the early days, no sewer or electrical lines existed. Residents, until the late 1930s, used outdoor toilets, kerosene lamps and wood- and coal-burning stoves.

Several businesses existed in The Flats. They included beauty shops, barbershops, grocery stores, a drugstore and others. The Blue Moon and Do Drop-In cafés remained popular for many years, as did Clara Shields Café and Hotel.

Dunbar School stood at Seventeenth Street and Avenue C. It opened in 1923 on a lot where an unnamed school had been located since 1920. William H. Wilson, who was the principal, his wife and Ella Carruthers

A current view looking east along Seventeenth Street in Lubbock, in the heart of what was The Flats neighborhood until the 1960s. *Courtesy Paul H. Carlson.*

were the teachers. In 1928, officials made additions to Dunbar School, and in 1930, it enrolled 227 students. In 1932, the year Lubbock ISD officials moved it to Date Avenue, Dunbar, with E.C. "Prof" Struggs as principal, held its first commencement as a high school. Six seniors received diplomas.

Several churches existed in The Flats. Mount Gilead Baptist Church was the first. Its members met in the home of Ida Stafford on Seventeenth Street and Avenue A before they acquired their own building. Others included Caldonia Baptist, Bethel African Methodist Episcopal Church and Mount Calvary Baptist.

Social life in The Flats, according to Roy Roberts and Katie Parks, "centered around a dance hall on Avenue A, and people would come from miles around to attend the dances." Many of the social activities, they write, "occurred through private house parties," but there were "style shows, musicals, and Christmas parties." Juneteenth, June 19—Texas Emancipation Day—was a major holiday with "a dance, picnics, speeches, and games."

Over the years, but especially after World War II, people left for other subdivisions, and The Flats became less attractive as a residential neighborhood. It fell apart with urban renewal in the 1960s, and today, the little tract stands forlorn and nearly empty.

Chapter 47

Clent Breedlove's Lubbock Airfield

John W. McCullough

Many legends have grown over the decades about a great man from Lubbock's aviation past named Clent Breedlove, but few people know exactly where his private airport was located during World War II. Although its official name was Commercial Airport, it became known as Breedlove Airport. Located at 2236 East Fiftieth Street, it stood about one-half mile east of the old Tahoka Highway (Quirt Avenue, now Martin Luther King Jr. Boulevard).

Breedlove Airport opened on December 19, 1941, just two weeks after the Japanese attacked Pearl Harbor, forcing the United States into war. However, since September 1939, Breedlove and his instructor airmen already had been busy training dozens of student pilots in the Civilian Pilot Training (CPT) program. They trained them at the older Lubbock Municipal Airport in a hangar that still stands south of the original brick hangar.

In October 1941, Breedlove and his wife, Aulyne, purchased 219 acres of land from Guy Patillo and moved into the two-story house located on the north-most part of the land facing East Fiftieth Street. At the time, East Fiftieth Street was a narrow dirt road that connected the old Tahoka Highway and the old Slaton Highway on the east, now called Southeast Drive.

The Breedloves paid Patillo about $29,000 for the land. They purchased it with a loan from a local bank with the note co-signed by their good friend Jimmy Vickers, another local aviator.

Clent Breedlove. *Courtesy John McCullough.*

Clent Breedlove built a large hangar and graded the runways. At first, he used an old windmill as the control tower. Eventually, he erected eight structures in proximity, and the buildings formed the working area of the airport.

Besides the original hangar, Breedlove constructed a shop, storage hangar, doping room, classroom, adjoining men's and women's restrooms, guardhouse and two-story administration building with a control tower on top. He later attached a café to the administration building's west side.

Breedlove Airport became a twenty-four-hour, all-weather facility with boundary lights and a beacon. There were also twenty "T" hangars alongside the northeast runway that private citizens might rent for storing their personal aircraft. Four large, graded runways existed. Two of them, a northeast–southwest runway and an east–west runway, crisscrossed immediately south of the headquarters complex. All runways were 300 feet wide, with the east–west runway the longest at 4,500 feet.

Shortly after his new facility opened, Breedlove moved his CPT program to it. As a result, during the war years (1942–45), Breedlove Airport was a busy place.

Then on February 6, 1943, Congressman George C. Mahon announced in the *Lubbock Morning Avalanche* that the United States Army Air Force (USAAF) would be locating a new training course in Lubbock, one called the 309th College Training Detachment (CTD). It became known as the Texas Tech Pre-flights program. Breedlove and his pilot-training company, Breedlove Aerial Services, became the civilian contractor for the training.

By June 1944, an estimated 3,750 student pilots of the 309th CTD had trained with Breedlove and his instructors, which now numbered over 30. While teaching pilots in the 309th CTD, Breedlove continued to train pilots in his own CPT program, with much of the training at Dagley Field, another local airport that he operated. Dagley Field stood at Thirty-Fourth Street and Quaker Avenue (formerly Dagley Road).

The Breedlove Airport was located at 2236 East Fiftieth in southeast Lubbock, pictured here in 1946. *Courtesy John McCullough.*

Although important for training military pilots, Breedlove Airport became a commercial airfield. The USAAF had taken over the Lubbock Municipal Airport to use in training glider pilots at South Plains Army Airfield (SPAAF).

For training several thousand pilots, Clent and Aulyne Breedlove received an estimated $1.2 million. In exchange, they covered expenses related to the training, including the salaries of the instructors and aircraft maintenance. The Breedloves operated under what was known as a "cost-plus contract" with the USAAF.

The Breedloves closed their airport in 1948 and, over subsequent years, sold sections of the land. Sometime between 1973 and 1975, a grass fire destroyed all structures at Breedlove Airport, including buildings being used as storage by Paul Bush of Lubbock Electric Company.

Today, an official marker from the Texas Historical Commission identifies the former location of Lubbock's Breedlove Airport.

Chapter 48

Lubbock's Major Military Bases of World War II

Don Abbe

In the late 1930s, as intra-European diplomatic and military relationships crumbled, the United States launched an aggressive program to increase the strength of its armed forces. Then, after World War II began in Europe, the U.S. military in 1940 and early 1941 grew massively. Congress established a peacetime draft, and after the Japanese attack at Pearl Harbor in December 1941, the military buildup accelerated at a frenetic pace.

A primary need was military training facilities, and by the hundreds, the federal government established such bases across the country. Lubbock became home to two major air-training bases for the U.S. Army Air Force: Lubbock Army Airfield and South Plains Army Airfield. The first, Lubbock Army Airfield, was established in June 1941 as part of the prewar defense mobilization program.

Located about ten miles west of Lubbock, it later became Reese Air Force Base. Ultimately, it reached about 1,600 acres in size. The army leased the lands from the City of Lubbock.

Construction began in August 1941. By early 1942, Lubbock Army Airfield contained over two hundred structures and three 6,500-foot runways. A steady stream of base personnel arrived in 1941, and the first class of trainees arrived in February 1942.

The facility was an Advanced Twin Engine Training site. Between February 1942 and September 1945, it produced over seven thousand pilots. These pilots eventually flew aircraft ranging from C-47s to B-29s, and they flew them in every corner of the world.

The flight line at Lubbock Army Airfield, later to become Reese Air Force Base, circa 1944. *Photo from Laney Lenox.*

The army air corps deactivated the airfield in September 1945. It closed on December 31, but it continued as a "stand-by" installation, which meant it remained in use by the U.S. military. National Guard and Reserve activities occurred at the airfield, and the barracks became housing units for veterans attending Texas Technological College on the GI Bill.

As the Cold War developed with the Soviet Union in the late 1940s, the U.S. Air Force in August 1949 reopened the facility as Reese Air Force Base. As a part of the reopening process, the City of Lubbock deeded the entire airfield to the U.S. government.

The new base, named for Augustus Reese of Shallowater, became one of the premier training fields for Advanced Multi-Engine training.

In early 1950, the first classes graduated from Reese Air Force Base. For thirty-seven years, U.S. Air Force pilots trained at Reese. The base closed in 1997.

The city's second major training installation, the South Plains Army Airfield (SPAAF), was established in 1942. In the early months of that year, the City of Lubbock offered the army use of its Municipal Airport, located north of the city at the current Preston Smith International Airport. The site contained almost 1,600 acres, with some newly completed concrete runways already in place. Also in place were a sheet metal hangar, a 1929 brick Municipal Airport hangar, a control tower and a manager's residence.

The airfield became a small city. Several thousand people lived and worked around the clock at SPAAF.

SPAAF was an "Advanced Training" base for the U.S. military's Combat Glider program. It became one of the premier bases in the national system.

By early 1943, the South Plains Army Airfield had become the only base in the large glider system where pilots received advanced training. Over 80 percent of the approximately six thousand World War II glider pilots trained at the facility.

But as the war wound down, the glider training facility's mission ended. SPAAF's last class graduated on January 15, 1945. With no other mission for the base, the army in February placed the airfield on its inactive list.

The City of Lubbock had agreed in 1942 to lease the property to the U.S. Army for one dollar per year. Among other things, the lease provided for the return of the base after the war—with or without the government's wartime improvements. Yet only after a thorny four-year struggle with the federal government did Lubbock get its airport back. As part of the return process, a new terminal building went up in 1950.

The building served as the Lubbock airport terminal until the mid-1970s. It now houses the Silent Wings Museum, dedicated to preserving the history of the World War II Glider Program.

Part VII
Bright Lights of the Llano

Citizens of Lubbock threw a great celebration in 1923 when they learned that the city had secured the location of a new major college, Texas Tech. They did it again, seventy years later, when their beloved Tech's women basketball team, the Lady Raiders, won the school's first national championship in any sport.

Those celebrations are only two of the bright lights of Llano Estacado history. In fact, in 1951, another event forever linked the word "lights" to Lubbock when observers spotted the "Lubbock Lights" in the evening sky.

Other lights brightened the heart of many cowboys at Christmas dances at isolated ranches across the region. In later years, flashing neon lights pointed the way to two of the region's most famous dance halls, the Cotton Club and the Palm Room, which provided great entertainment for decades.

Buddy Holly's rise to fame in the 1950s made Lubbock shine brighter. At the National Cowgirl Hall of Fame in Fort Worth, a museum that had its beginning at Hereford, brilliant lights now shine on famous cowgirls. And one of Lubbock's brightest lights was one of its most dedicated teachers, Mae Simmons.

Collectively, these stories are illustrative of the many bright lights of the Llano Estacado.

Chapter 49

Early Christmas Celebrations around the Caprock

David J. Murrah

Christmas can be a lonely time, especially for those who have to live or work in isolated places. But the early residents of the Llano Estacado proved resourceful and made Christmas the highlight of the year.

One of the earliest Christmas celebrations was also one of the most exciting. In 1872, Captain Jack Elgin and a survey party of about thirty men were caught in a winter storm at Christmas near the Double Mountains southwest of present-day Aspermont. The blowing snow pushed a large herd of bison and an abundance of other game right into their camp two days before Christmas, and the men did some quick hunting. As a result, their Christmas Day meal was a banquet. "I think we had fourteen varieties of meat," Elgin remembered, "buffalo, antelope, deer, bear, rabbit, prairie dog, possum…turkey, goose, ducks, prairie chickens, curlew, quail, and other birds."

Elgin also said that his cook mixed vanilla oil with condensed milk and water and left the mixture in the snow overnight to make ice cream. He recalled that Christmas day with great fondness: "No prince, potentate, or magnate ever sat down to such a feast."

By the 1880s, area ranches had begun hosting Christmas celebrations. In January 1882, W.B. Slaughter and his wife, Anna, hosted a delayed Christmas dance at their ranch in southeastern Crosby County, northwest of present-day Spur. The three-day event attracted more than thirty cowboys and nine women from all the surrounding counties. The Slaughters served barbecued beef, ham from wild hogs, deer and antelope, jelly, doughnuts and fried pies and cake.

Cowboy photographer Erwin E. Smith (1886–1947) captured this ranch dance, unhampered by lack of women, circa 1910. *Photo gelatin dry plate negative; Erwin E. Smith Collection of the Library of Congress on Deposit at and courtesy of the Amon Carter Museum of American Art, Fort Worth, Texas; LC.S6.058.*

Rollie Burns recalled the fortitude of the women who attended: "Three nights and two days—quadrilles, waltzes, schottisches, and polkas. I wondered how the women stood it. With the men it was different. There were three times as many of them as women; consequently they got to rest about two-thirds of the time."

In March 1882, the new town of Dockum, north of Spur, held its delayed Christmas dance. The celebration, postponed awaiting completion of Dockum's new store, included a cedar Christmas tree that the cowboys cut in the breaks below the caprock. "The [party] was as big a success as if it had taken place on schedule," Rollie Burns recalled. "Everyone was in a festive mood....While the boys were waiting turns in the sets, they hustled the coffee pot and smoked cigarettes, occasionally taking a Christmas 'nip' from a bottle of Four Roses."

Settlers at the new community of Estacado had used a cedar tree for its first Christmas celebration in 1879. But in the years that followed, towns on the treeless plains had to be more inventive. One community used a yucca plant for a tree. At Brownfield, men built a tree from two-by-four boards, and women covered it with green calico, with a yucca at the base. Seminole's residents also built a lumber frame but covered it with cedar clippings. People decorated trees with handmade items and always included strings of popcorn, cranberries and occasionally cookies. Schoolchildren would also make paper chains to hang on the community tree.

In 1883, the Matador Ranch dance attracted cowboys from nearly one hundred miles away, even though there were only three women in attendance. The manager's wife, "Lizzie" Campbell, prepared wild turkey "larded liberally" with strips of bacon from wild hogs killed on the ranch. She also prepared dressing, antelope stew, venison steak, boiled ham, wild rice, canned corn, apple pies made from dried apples, doughnuts and wild plum jelly. But her big hit was popcorn balls. "I had brought out with me from the east some popcorn," Lizzie remembered. "I think the cowboys really enjoyed these more than anything."

An annual Christmas dance at Anson in Jones County became popular. Held for about eight years in M.G. Rhodes's Star Hotel, the "Cowboy's Christmas Ball," as it was called, in the 1880s attracted men, women and children from far beyond tiny Anson. After the hotel burned in 1891, the dance occurred only intermittently until Leonora Barrett and friends revived it in 1934.

Drought in the late 1880s sometimes made food supplies scarce. On the Lowe farm near Plainview, Mrs. Lowe had saved two eggs from her single hen for Christmas baking before a coyote claimed her last chicken. She baked a one-egg cake and planned to carry the other egg to her neighbor, Mrs. Portwood, who had none, on Christmas. But a cowboy from a distant ranch saved the day. At midnight on Christmas Eve, he arrived at the Portwood farm with a dozen eggs he had purchased en route, carefully wrapped in a red bandana that he carried on his arm for hours while in the saddle. When Mrs. Lowe arrived the next morning, she found plenty of cakes already prepared for the Christmas gathering.

The first community Christmas in Lubbock was a polite affair, held in a blacksmith shop in old north Lubbock in 1890. It featured a mixed quartet, organ music and games "that had little action so we would not raise too much dust," recalled Mrs. W.N. Green. The following year, the celebration moved to the new courthouse, but as new churches were built, they staged their own observances, and the community-wide Christmas celebration faded away.

Chapter 50

Lubbock's Original Cotton Club

Ashley Pettiet

The Lubbock Cotton Club was a ballroom, concert arena and dance hall. It was a venue for big bands, country and western performers, rock-and-roll artists and all musicians who fell in between.

The Cotton Club accomplished what most dance halls of its era could not fathom: for four decades, from 1938 to 1980, it appealed to all of Lubbock's social and racial classes. Beyond being the venue for the popular artists of the time, the club interacted with the local community in various ways. It hosted the Junior Welfare League's Charity Ball in 1946, for example, and it was Lubbock's first, and for many years only, integrated dance hall. With such a diverse level of community involvement, the Cotton Club engaged and influenced both the Lubbock community and the larger South Plains region.

The Cotton Club opened in Lubbock on November 11, 1938. Lubbock's newest nightspot, housed in a renovated army Quonset hut, stood west of Railroad Avenue (present-day Southeast Drive) north of Fiftieth Street.

On opening night, as the club's first entertainers, manager Clyde M. Trusty booked Frank "Deacon" Murino and his Men about Town, along with Adelle Kastle, a proclaimed female violinist and "songster" of swing, a popular genre at the time.

The *Lubbock Avalanche Journal*'s advertisement for the club proclaimed it "Lubbock's finest dining and dancing palace." With over two thousand feet of hardwood floor space that was as "smooth as glass," the Cotton Club permitted over one hundred customers for dinner and at the same time allowed almost five hundred people to dance.

Nonetheless, with dances held twice a week and with the largest capacity of any dance hall in West Texas, the Cotton Club during its first several years faced a problem. In the last years of the Great Depression, Lubbock's population did not contain enough citizens in socioeconomic circles affluent enough to support big orchestras every week. Or, as bandleader Tommy Hancock, who owned the club years later, indelicately put it, Lubbock in 1940 did not have enough "classy" people to sustain a six-hundred-person-capacity dance hall.

To encourage greater attendance, in 1941 Trusty began to expand the club's musical offerings. He brought in country and western dance orchestras. One of the first such bands was Bob Wills with his Texas Playboys.

According to I.G. Holmes, the club photographer from 1949 to 1953, Trusty in 1952 sold the dance hall to Ralph Lowe for $500. During Lowe's ownership (1952–58), the Cotton Club reached a high point in its popularity. Lowe's ability to book some of the biggest performers of country and western music as well as some of the pioneers of a new genre—rock-and-roll—gave the Cotton Club respectability. It became a favorite entertainment venue, especially as rock-and-roll expanded.

Other ballrooms in the city attempted to mimic the club's appeal to people who enjoyed a mix of country-dance and rock-and-roll. They had minimal success.

The Cotton Club dominated the dance hall scene, and in the mid-1950s, it emerged as a West Texas and, to some extent, national leader in the cultivation of rock-and-roll music.

From his first visit to Lubbock on January 2, 1955, Elvis Presley enjoyed huge popularity. He first appeared at the Fair Park Coliseum with a group of country and western artists. After the performance, Presley went to the Cotton Club, where he treated fans to a spontaneous and unscheduled performance.

Six weeks later, on February 13, he returned to the Cotton Club. This time, Presley performed on Teen Night. Lubbock's Buddy Holly, a Teen Night regular, met the rock-and-roll star. The Cotton Club meeting was a life-altering experience for Holly. It changed his music.

In August 1956, Little Richard, another rock-and-roll pioneer, came to the Cotton Club. At his performance, a crowd numbering well over the club's six-hundred-person-capacity showed up. Some people moved outside, and fighting broke out. Fearing the fights would move inside his club, Lowe called a stop to Richard's concert.

The incident gave the Cotton Club a regrettable reputation. Afterward, one Lubbock grandmother warned her grandchildren, "You go to that place and you will get your gizzard cut out."

Still, the Cotton Club succeeded and even gained in popularity. But its very success contributed to its decline. Because it enjoyed a monopoly on big artists coming through the area, rivals burned it. Such a fate was in keeping with 1950s-era dance halls. Although authorities filed no charges, most people believe a competitor burned the Cotton Club, an event that happened more than once.

The old Cotton Club was gone. But a new club under different owners soon appeared southeast of Lubbock on the Slaton Highway (U.S. 84). Like the burned-out old one, the new club continued to influence South Plains dance halls and music culture. As it did, the original Cotton Club became a wonderful memory.

Chapter 51

THE LUBBOCK LIGHTS SIGHTING, 1951

Meredith McClain

The term "Lubbock Lights" keeps popping up in the name of events and other promotions, all because of a most unusual phenomenon. It began on August 25, 1951, when three Texas Technological College professors sitting on the front patio of Dr. Wilbur I. Robinson's adobe home on Twenty-Fourth Street observed an arc of green lights speeding soundlessly far overhead. Shortly afterward, the lights, or a second bank of them, came again.

The unusual nocturnal displays, which others in the city witnessed and from time to time saw over several weeks, quickly became part of the UFO phenomenon sweeping the country. Numerous sightings of UFOs in the American Southwest had begun in 1947, and the U.S. Air Force responded by establishing a special "Project Saucer" to investigate all reports. In 1952, the air force downgraded the status of the special saucer project to "a standard intelligence function," but it invited "all citizens to report their sightings to the nearest air force installation." By then, the air force had dismissed as natural phenomena all but thirty-four of hundreds of such cases.

Also in 1952, the then popular and influential *Life* magazine published a lead article on the flying saucers topic, titled "There Is a Case for Interplanetary Saucers." After a year of sifting through many reports filed with the air force, *Life* went to press. Its long article focused on the essential details of what it considered ten of the most formidable UFO cases, starting with the "Lubbock Lights."

The strange lights of 1951 and the *Life* article in 1952 put Lubbock in the national consciousness. The three Tech professors were largely responsible.

The men on Robinson's patio that August evening included Robinson, a geologist; William L. Ducker, head of petroleum engineering; and Dr. A. Gus Oberg, professor of chemical engineering. The men had just settled in for their weekly "Saturday Evening Seminar." They had enjoyed their Saturday patio visits for many years. The only rule for their wide-ranging discussions was no talk of religion, politics or women.

Sometimes Dr. Robinson produced a homemade pie, baked in a metal box oven placed onto one of his gas burners. The dial next to the little peephole window in the oven went only from "off "to "on."

Professor Ducker had just made medical history, being the first human to survive surgery for Crohn's disease. He eased himself carefully into his lawn chair, facing northeast, toward downtown Lubbock. Perhaps Robinson passed some pie and the conversation began.

Then suddenly, as darkness settled in, Ducker leaped from his chair, pointed wildly toward the sky and shouted, "What the hell is that?" All three men observed the arc of green lights speeding soundlessly high overhead.

In the vague hope of a returning apparition, the professors snuffed out their pipes and cigar and trained their sharpened vision on the clear night sky. Sure enough, it came over again—or a second formation flew over.

The *Life* magazine article stated, "The Lubbock Lights, flying in formation, are considered by the Air Force the most unexplainable phenomena yet observed."

Certainly, the credibility of observations of the three witnesses (all scientists) from the adobe house patio is an essential factor in the air force's judgment of the lights as a "most unexplainable" phenomenon.

Also important were sightings by people from throughout the city, all confirming what the Tech professors had seen. A youthful Kenneth Davis, who would later become a Texas Tech English professor, saw the lights while at a drive-in theater on the Idalou Highway.

Plus there were photographs. On August 30, eighteen-year-old Carl Hart Jr. took five images of the V-shaped lights as they sped across the night sky. The college professors suspected Hart's photos were fakes of some kind, but the air force upheld them as plausible.

Because they could measure neither the size nor distance of the formations they saw in the night sky, the professors could not determine the objects' speed. The best estimate they and others offered was that, considering the arc and silence of the objects, the lights were fifty thousand

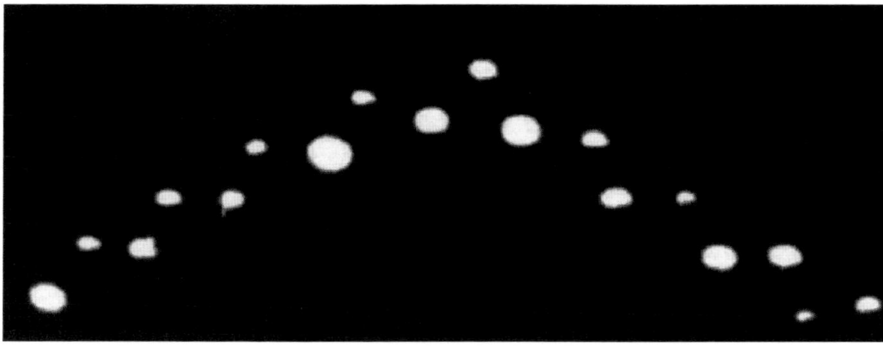

The 1951 Lubbock Lights, as photographed by Texas Tech student William Hart Jr. Whether the picture is authentic has been debated for decades. *Courtesy Meredith McClain.*

feet in the air. In which case, they guessed, the lights were moving at eighteen thousand miles per hour.

Or perhaps, as some people have speculated, the arc of green lights represented nothing more than migrating birds reflecting a new lighting system installed along Nineteenth Street near Texas Technological College.

Whatever the case, in April 2015, former president of Texas Tech University Dr. Duane Nellis and Andy Wilkinson of Tech's Southwest Collection organized an event to honor local musicians and called it the Lubbock Lights Musical Festival. The first honorees included Wade Bowen, Butch Hancock, Terri Hendrix and Lloyd Maines. The celebrated musicians all represent today's "Lubbock Lights."

Chapter 52

Mae Simmons

June Steele

Mae Simmons (1909–1981) taught social studies in Lubbock's schools for many years. Born Mae Thomas near Dawson, Texas, in Navarro County, she was the granddaughter of slaves. Her paternal grandfather had moved the family from Tennessee to Texas, acquiring enough land to support through cotton farming his children and grandchildren.

Contracting polio at age six drastically changed Mae's life. It left her without the use of her right arm. Mae traveled with her mother to hospitals throughout Texas and as far away as St. Louis, Missouri, seeking treatment, but to no avail. Because her arm remained paralyzed and thus excused her from intense manual labor, she concentrated on learning and education.

At age thirteen, Mae began helping at Sunday school. She attended elementary school in Dawson, eventually graduating from high school in Wichita Falls, Texas, to where her parents had moved in 1927. Mae Thomas was eligible for educational assistance from the Texas State Rehabilitation Association for Crippled Children. The organization paid for her first two years of study at Prairie View State Normal and Industrial College, the state's teachers' college for black students.

Knowing that her family could not afford the tuition for the remaining two years, Mae accepted a teaching job in a one-room schoolhouse in Henrietta, twenty miles southeast of Wichita Falls. African American children from the first through the ninth grade attended the school in Henrietta, and Mae taught there for four years, describing it as "the best experience I ever had." Because their ages differed so widely, each

Mae Simmons taught in the Lubbock school system for nearly forty years. *Courtesy Southwest Collection, Texas Tech University.*

child had to be taught individually, creating, according to Mae, a truly rewarding, fulfilling learning environment.

During her four years in Henrietta, Mae met her husband, Ira Simmons, eventually following him to Lubbock, where they married in 1939. For the first four months of the marriage, Mae Simmons retained her job in Henrietta, traveling back and forth by bus to Lubbock, until her husband asked her to resign.

During her first two years in Lubbock, Simmons served as a substitute teacher at the Dunbar School, the all-black school, where she met principal and teacher Edward Struggs. Because the black student population was growing, Struggs asked Simmons to return to college to complete her bachelor's degree. Upon gaining the consent of her husband, Simmons headed to Houston College for Negroes (Texas Southern University), where she finished her bachelor's degree in education in only twelve months.

In 1942, Simmons was back in Lubbock and teaching full time as a fourth grade teacher at Dunbar. In some ways, the experience was full of frustrations, for her African American student population faced harsh living conditions. Many such students, including those from migrant farm worker families, attended school sporadically, and they often left town after the fall harvest. Some were part of families unable to afford frame houses. They often purchased or leased vacant lots and built dugouts on them.

Partly as a result, teachers of black children never knew how many of their students would make it through each term.

In spite of the obstacles, the permanent African American population continued to grow, as did the need for African American educators. Simmons recognized the need. "I attended school in Houston," she said, "and could have gone to work there. But there was so much work to be done here in Lubbock. The children came from families who needed a lot of help."

Determined to improve herself, along with the state of black education in Lubbock, Mae Simmons left Texas briefly to pursue graduate work. As an African American and thus prohibited from graduate study at any of the universities in Texas, Simmons in 1946 set out for the University of Iowa and returned to Lubbock with her master's degree in education a year later.

An advanced degree in the 1940s set Simmons above a large majority of public school teachers in the nation. Many of her siblings and cousins urged Simmons to relocate to South Texas to be with family.

Mae Simmons stayed on in Lubbock, eventually becoming the principal at Ella Iles Elementary. An increase in Lubbock's black teacher salaries in the early 1950s further raised her commitment to the community.

In addition to her years of combined service as classroom teacher and principal in three Lubbock schools, Simmons volunteered extensively in many civic organizations, including the Lubbock Planning Council, Lubbock Cancer Society, the United Way, YWCA, YMCA, Girl Scouts and Boy Scouts.

Simmons's teaching career in Lubbock extended over thirty years. She retired in 1972, stating problems with her health, particularly regarding her disabled arm.

In 1970, the City of Lubbock dedicated a park and community center to her, a monument to her service. Today, the Mae Simmons Community Center, Mae Simmons Senior Citizen Center and Mae Simmons Pool all sit proudly atop the rolling hills overlooking the Upper North Fork of the Double Mountain Fork of the Brazos River and Canyon Lake near Oak Avenue and Martin Luther King Boulevard.

Chapter 53

Margaret Formby and the National Cowgirl Hall of Fame

David J. Murrah

The visions of West Texans can become big. What began in 1975 as a dream to recognize the accomplishments of rodeo cowgirls has become the internationally known National Cowgirl Hall of Fame, housed in a beautiful thirty-three-thousand-square-foot museum located in the heart of the Fort Worth Museum District.

But it all began in Hereford in 1975. As a part of the city's planning for the 1976 American Bicentennial Celebration, promoters in the chamber of commerce, headed by manager Bill Albracht, envisioned a hall of fame for rodeo cowgirls that would complement a local all-girl rodeo.

It was chamber member Roy Faubion who initially raised the idea. As a fan of the National Cowboy Hall of Fame in Oklahoma City, he discovered that there was not a similar museum for cowgirls. "Why isn't there one?" Faubion asked. He envisioned a cowgirl museum that would "be like the cowboy hall in scope," he told writer Jimmie Hurley in the summer of 1975, "but not be a copy of it. We wanted the cowgirl hall to have a personality of its own."

The idea caught on quickly. Albracht recruited a board of directors, and Faubion became its president. In May 1975, the board temporarily located the Hall of Fame in the basement of the new Deaf Smith County Library and erected a large billboard at a proposed building site in Hereford.

On May 18, 1975, the hall's first three inductees were presented at the final performance of the rodeo, each representing different eras of women's rodeo history: Jackie Worthington, Elenor "Sissy" Thurman and Alice Greenough

Roy Faubion, the first president of the National Cowgirl Hall of Fame, and board member Margaret Clemmons stand at the proposed site of the Hereford museum in 1975. *Courtesy National Cowgirl Museum and Hall of Fame, Fort Worth, Texas.*

Norr. Worthington had won twenty-three world rodeo championships in her thirteen-year career, Thurman was the nation's top barrel racer in the late 1940s and Norr was an international rodeo star and trick rider who had also created the sport of barrel racing.

The all-girl rodeo continued only for a few years, but the Cowgirl Hall of Fame survived through some difficult times.

By 1978, Margaret Formby, wife of Hereford radio station owner Clint Formby, had become executive director of the Hall of Fame. A native of Van Horn and a 1950 graduate of Texas Tech University, she had been a charter member of the Texas Tech Rodeo Association and the first Miss Texas Tech. Under her leadership, the Hall of Fame grew slowly but was large enough by 1982 to move to a donated six-thousand-square-foot house on the outskirts of Hereford.

By the end of 1993, the National Cowgirl Hall of Fame included 115 inductees, a list that included not only rodeo stars but also notable writers, western entertainers and ranch women. But the museum had outgrown its Hereford home. By that time, its collections included thousands of items, including saddles, costumes, Patsy Montana's rhinestone hat and much more.

Formby and her board of directors knew that the hall deserved more than what Hereford could provide. The group sought solicitations from larger cities to host the museum. "We'd go for stretches, where for days on end, [no visitors] would come," she related to a reporter in 2002. After entertaining inquiries and bids from more than thirty cities, the board accepted Fort Worth's offer in 1994, and the Hall of Fame relocated, leaving a bittersweet feeling with its founders. "It's kind of like having a child and having to give that child up," Formby later explained.

Hereford's Margaret Formby. *Courtesy National Cowgirl Museum and Hall of Fame, Fort Worth, Texas.*

In 1994, the Hall of Fame inducted Margaret Formby into the hall because of her vision and long dedication to its development.

In 2002, the museum opened in its sparkling new multimillion-dollar facility adjacent to Fort Worth's other prestigious museums. The Hall of Fame now includes 228 honorees; many, such as Sacagawea, artist Georgia O'Keeffe, writer Laura Ingalls Wilder, sharpshooter Annie Oakley, actress Dale Evans and Supreme Court justice Sandra Day O'Connor, may not have been rodeo performers, but they possessed strong associations with cowgirls, ranching or the American West.

It also includes, in addition to Formby, nine other longtime natives or residents of the Llano Estacado: rancher and rodeo star Fern Sawyer of Tatum, New Mexico (inducted in 1976); barrel racer Mike Reid Settle of Tulia (1977); author Mamie Burns of Dickens and Lubbock (1981); Margaret Harper of Canyon, founder of the outdoor musical *Texas* (1981); rancher Dessie Sawyer of Tatum (1981); rancher and rodeo star Mary Ellen "Dude" Barton of Flomot (1984); horse trainer and equestrian judge Suzanne Jones of Tatum (1999); livestock auctioneer Norma Sanders of Texico, New Mexico (1994); and rancher Wilma Powell of Plains (2008).

In 2000, because of her leadership and work with the Hall of Fame, the *Amarillo Globe-News* named Margaret Formby to its list of one hundred of the most important "History Makers of the High Plains." Only seventeen women were included in the list.

Sadly, as a result of a fall in her home, Formby died in 2003. However, she lived to see that the Hereford vision was fulfilled in a way that far exceeded the original dream, as thousands annually continue to visit the National Cowgirl Hall of Fame in Fort Worth.

Chapter 54

The Palm Room

Christena Stephens

Imagine a Polynesian island paradise in Lubbock County—a place where, upon arrival, you are saluted by a seven-foot-tall tiki statue. Then, as you enter the building, bamboo walls, coconuts, paper lanterns, palm trees and a lava waterfall greet you. A glassed-in rainforest section holds a banana tree, parakeets and cockatoos. At its center, the large, remarkable room holds a revolving bandstand, highlighted by a beautiful pine dance floor.

This island paradise was the Palm Room. Located east of Lubbock on the Idalou Highway, it had once been part of a large dairy barn. J.P. "Jim" Hallmark, a longtime Lubbock County resident, and his wife, Oleta Price, owned the building and farm associated with it. In the 1950s, when the Hallmarks could find no buyer for their farm, they converted the large barn into a "club."

The Palm Room officially opened on September 14, 1956. It became West Texas's finest ballroom and reportedly sold the best steaks. Orchestra music filled the Palm Room, with local bands playing to guests, along with appearances from the Barons, Chuck Cabot, Larry Fontaine, Harry James and Tony Douglas and the Shrimpers. The dress code was always semi-formal. No blue jeans were allowed. Women wore long dresses, and men wore tuxes or suits. The "dry" precinct in which it stood made the Palm Room a BYOB establishment. Patrons often kept onsite liquor lockers to store their alcohol. From the original converted barn, the ballroom grew to twenty-five thousand square feet. In 1967, the Hallmarks added the Tropics Club, giving members a year-round indoor swimming pool.

Dorothy and Jimmy Blakley with Merle Haggard at the Palm Room, circa 1972. *Courtesy Eaton Martin-Vader Company.*

After Jim died in 1968, Oleta operated the Palm Room for a time by herself, but in 1971, she sold it to Jimmy and Dorothy Blakley of Roswell, New Mexico. Recording artists, the Blakleys often worked with Norman Petty in Clovis. Their record labels included Mercury, Starday, Dixie "D" Darsa, Midas and United Artists. The change in ownership shifted the island paradise music from orchestra-based to country/country swing. Initially, attendance fell off a bit, but the Palm Room soon grew again into a popular place for dining and dancing.

Everyone in the Blakley family worked at the club. Each member was a singer and a musician. Dorothy loved to cook and was found in the kitchen as much as on the bandstand. The family captivated club-goers. People danced to their music played on steel guitars, bass guitars, guitars, fiddles, banjos, organ, piano and drums.

The Palm Room could cater and serve up to one thousand people. A back bar sold sodas, ginger ales, tomato juices and buckets of ice, as well as party trays with homemade onion dip.

Bill Winner recalled, "It was such a cool island paradise feel in the middle of a cotton patch. It impressed me as a youngster new to the club life."

The Blakleys' daughter Debbie Blakley-Eaton has strong memories of the Palm Room. She can still see the faces, smell the rooms, sense the ambiance of lights and decor and hear the music. She remembers the clamor of the kitchen and the business of the folks filing in and out of the front door. She can still feel the eeriness of being in the building late at night with her dad as he methodically made his rounds with a .38 pistol on his belt. "He was a gentle man," she said, "but no one's fool."

The bands and the dances attracted people to the Palm Room. The music of such entertainers as the Sons of the Pioneers, Hank Williams, Sammi Smith, Janis Joplin, Anne Murray, Ray Price, Bill Anderson and Glen Miller echoed from the walls. Merle Haggard stopped by once for a visit.

Jimmy Blakley loved fulfilling written song requests scribbled on napkins and singing multitudes of "Happy Birthday" and the "Anniversary Waltz" for patrons.

The Blakleys were passionate about their music, and the Palm Room gave them a platform to perform and entertain. As recording artists, their career spanned the years from the mid-1950s to the mid-1970s. The couple also recorded at the Palm Room on their PR International label.

The Blakley musical legacy continues. Three of their children became musicians.

Dorothy died in 1983. Jimmy kept the Palm Room operating for two more years before he sold it.

The building stills stands and the dance floor inside remains, nostalgic reminders of the Palm Room's former life and the dreams of bringing Polynesian décor, lively music, popular dancing and great food to the Llano Estacado's dusty plains.

Chapter 55

Buddy Holly's Lubbock in the Late 1950s

Paul H. Carlson

During the 1950s, Buddy Holly (1936–1959) was a teenager in Lubbock. He was a part of the local music scene, and he became a big part of the city's music tradition.

That tradition is often full of energy; it is often hardworking, plain-folk music—like Terry Allen's "Amarillo Highway." It is, while acknowledging the superb compositions and performances from Texas Tech University's music department, sometimes related to the soft vulgarity of Roy Orbison's "I Drove All Night" or Holly's "Oh Boy." Like Mac Davis's "It's Hard to Be Humble," it grabs your attention. In a socially and culturally conservative Lubbock of the 1950s, how was it possible for young Holly and such others as Waylon Jennings, Sonny Curtis, Joe B. Mauldin, Virgil Johnson, Niki Sullivan, Glen Hardin and Tommy Hancock to produce their special music so full of energy and attention-grabbing lyrics?

Lubbock in the 1950s was in a boom period of growth. Its population increased from 72,000 in 1950 to almost 130,000 in 1960. It was energetic, self-confident and prosperous. It had three high schools, but two more would be built in the next decade. It had a bulging university in Texas Tech and a fledgling college in Lubbock Christian, which opened in 1957.

In Buddy Holly's high school days, one of Lubbock's newest and perhaps most fashionable housing subdivisions was O'Neil Terrace, located west of Avenue Q and north of Thirty-Fourth Street—across Avenue Q from present O.L. Slaton Jr. High School. People of wealth and position still lived along West Broadway, and Nineteenth Street was attracting people who sought large homes. In 1955, Buddy lived at 1906 Twenty-Fourth Street, but his family moved often. In the 1950s, Lubbock's downtown district was still viable and busy, but Thirty-Fourth Street was attracting attention as an important shopping area. Fiftieth Street in 1950 "was an unpaved, rutted street being considered as the outer loop for the city." South of Fiftieth Street spread cotton fields, empty lots and playa lakes.

In 1959, Monterrey and Caprock shopping centers opened along Fiftieth near Boston and Flint, and housing stretched several blocks south of there. No Loop 289 existed in the 1950s, Slide Road was far out in the country and plans for the South Plains Shopping Mall were not yet on the drawing board.

Poster promoting Elvis Presley concert at Lubbock's Fair Park Coliseum, 1955. One of the opening groups was the duo of Buddy and Bob, i.e., Buddy Holly and Bob Montgomery, who would later form the Crickets. *Courtesy Southwest Collection, Texas Tech University.*

In the late 1950s, high school students drag-raced their cars along a dirt- and gravel-based Eighty-Second Street westward from College (now University) Avenue. The dam at Buffalo Springs Lake was begun in the 1950s, and in 1960, Buffalo Springs Lake opened as a public recreation area.

High school and college students, perhaps including Buddy Holly, Jerry Allison and Peggy Sue Gerron, had for years gone out to Buffalo Springs and Ransom Canyon to swim; to test their automobiles on the area's winding, hilly roads; to drink some beer; to hold hands; and to listen on the car radio to Elvis Presley, Chuck Berry, Muddy Waters, Bill Haley and the Comets or other early rock-and-roll favorites.

In the 1950s, teenagers gathered at the Hi-D-Ho Drive In on Third and University and at the Village Mill, once located across from Jones AT&T Stadium in the old Town & Country Shopping Center. Young people "made the drag" as they drove their cars north on University to the Hi-D-Ho, turned right into the famous drive-in and drove around it and back out to University. They crossed University Avenue and drove through the alley behind the Town & Country and followed the alley west to the Village Mill. Or they drove through the Town & Country Shopping Center parking lot to stop and visit with others before turning back to the Hi-D-Ho or a rival drive-in nearby.

No Lubbock Civic Center existed in Buddy Holly's high school days. The Lubbock Auditorium and Coliseum were completed about 1956. Thus it was that in the mid-1950s, the Fair Park Coliseum on the South Plains Fair Grounds and the Cotton Club near Fiftieth Street and Southeast Drive attracted large, receptive crowds to hear the touring musicians who performed in Lubbock. Elvis Presley was among them. Presley played at both the Fair Park Coliseum and the Cotton Club in 1955, and Buddy Holly and Bob Montgomery opened for him.

In short, during the 1950s, as the roots of modern rock-and-roll music sent up powerful shoots, Buddy Holly's Lubbock grew with the same vigor, energy and spirit as its music.

Chapter 56

Texas Tech's National Basketball Championship, 1993

David J. Murrah

Texas Tech's 1993 national championship in women's basketball was meant to be, because the program was built on the champion competitive spirit that has always been a part of life on the Llano Estacado.

In the early 1950s, the Panhandle-Plains region quickly became the dominant region in Texas girls' basketball. Prior to 1992, its teams had captured the state crown in one division or more in thirty-seven of forty years.

In 1987, high school teams from Morton, Sudan, Slaton, Levelland and Plainview did the unimaginable; they all swept the state tournament crowns. Four years later, in 1991, Nazareth, Abernathy, Tulia, Levelland and Amarillo's Tascosa High repeated the feat.

It was Wayland Baptist College in Plainview that first took advantage of the regional basketball talent. At the insistence of members of Wayland's girls' basketball club, the school began playing AAU basketball in 1947, and its teams soon became the famous Hutcherson Flying Queens. Coached by Harley Redin and led by Dimmitt star Lometa Odem, the Queens from 1953 to 1958 fashioned an unprecedented 131-game win streak, the most ever in any sport. That record came to an end in Lubbock on March 20, 1958, when the Queens lost to Nashville Business College, 46–42, before six thousand fans at the Municipal Coliseum, probably the largest crowd ever to see a women's game to that time.

The creation of Title IX by Congress in 1972 dramatically changed the landscape for women's sports. Big schools, like Texas Tech, were required to provide equal opportunity for women's sports, and soon all were nationally competing for recruits.

Texas Tech fielded its first competitive team in 1975 with a schedule that was strikingly similar to the inaugural 1925 football season. The Lady Raiders played primarily junior colleges and small schools from the area. They lost their first game to Snyder's Western Texas Junior College, 83–40, and, a month later, won their first, a 70–66 win over Texas Women's University of Denton. They finished the 1975–76 season with a 14-16 record. They also lost to the Flying Queens, 106–30.

But it was a Flying Queen who transformed Texas Tech's basketball. Marsha Sharp, a product of Tulia's basketball program, played her freshman year for the Queens and became coach of their JV team, the Queen Bees, as a junior, learning coaching from future Hall of Famers Harley Redin and Dean Reese. She graduated from Wayland in 1974 and coached for six years at Lockney. In 1982, she became Tech's assistant coach and then head coach in 1983. It was the perfect match.

"I understand West Texas," Sharp told a reporter for *Texas Monthly* in 2005. "I am West Texas. It's my home. My dad was a Tech graduate. I can remember…sitting in the living room with him, listening to Jack Dale calling Texas Tech basketball games on the radio. Or watching Donny Anderson play football. For me it was the ultimate compliment to get to coach at Tech."

Under Sharp, in March 1984, the Lady Raiders made their first NCAA tournament appearance but lost to traditional powerhouse Louisiana Tech in the first round. They returned in 1986 and again in 1990, only to lose in the first round.

The 1990–91 season became the breakout year. That season, the Lady Raiders beat Texas 63–61 in the conference tournament after having lost thirty-seven straight to the Longhorns. Although Tech lost in the finals to Arkansas two days later and to Nevada–Las Vegas in the first round of the NCAA tourney, the Lady Raiders had finally broken the dominance of the Longhorns.

The 1991–92 season set the stage for the championship year. The Lady Raiders won the conference tourney with a win over Texas and then advanced to the second round of the NCAA before losing to Stanford. They finished with a best-ever 27-5 season.

With ten returning from that record-setting season, the Lady Raiders in 1992–93 seemed destined for greatness, but early losses to Stanford and Utah, coupled with a conference loss to Texas, raised eyebrows. But led by seniors Sheryl Swoopes from Brownfield and Krista Kirkland of Spearman,

The Lady Raiders were led to the national championship by Sheryl Swoopes, *top left*, and Krista Kirkland, *top right*. *Courtesy Southwest Collection, Texas Tech University*.

the Lady Raiders won eighteen straight to move into the finals of the NCAA tournament against Ohio State. In that game, Swoopes scored 47 points, including a lay-up and a foul shot with less than a minute remaining, to give the Lady Raiders a 7-point lead. They hung on to win 84–82.

More than forty thousand fans packed Jones Stadium to welcome home the Lady Raiders.

In a sense, it took the Lady Raiders only eleven years to win a national championship, as the NCAA began offering a national tournament in 1982. But that path was shorter because it passed through the halls of the great high school basketball programs on the plains, at places like Dimmitt, Canyon, Nazareth and Levelland, and on the court of Wayland Baptist University, where Marsha Sharp learned to coach.

Selected Bibliography

Abbe, Donald, Paul H. Carlson and David J. Murrah. *Lubbock and the South Plains: An Illustrated History*. 2nd ed. Tarzana, CA: Preferred Marketing, 1995.

Blodgett, Jan. *Land of Bright Promise: Advertising the Texas Panhandle and South Plains*. Austin: University of Texas Press, 1988.

Bogener, Stephen, and William Tydeman, eds. *Llano Estacado: An Island in the Sky*. Introduction by Barry Lopez. Lubbock: Texas Tech University Press, 2011.

Brink, Pamela, Cindy Martin, and Daniel Sanchez. *Images of America: Lubbock*. Charleston, SC: Arcadia Publishing, 2013.

Carlson, Paul H. *The Centennial History of Lubbock: Hub City of the Plains*. Virginia Beach, VA: Donning Company, Publishers, 2008.

———. *Deep Time and the Texas High Plains: History and Geology*. Lubbock: Texas Tech University Press, 2005.

Carr, Joe, and Alan Munde. *Prairie Nights: The Story of Country Music in West Texas*. Lubbock: Texas Tech University Press, 1995.

Cavazos, Lauro F., with Gene B. Preuss. *A Kineno's Journey: On Family, Learning, and Public Service*. Lubbock: Texas Tech University Press, 2016.

Connor, Seymour V., ed. *Builders of the Southwest*. Lubbock: Southwest Collection, Texas Tech University, 1959.

Cutter, Paul F. *Early Lubbock: A Cultural View*. Austin, TX: Eakin Press, 1991.

Eaves, Charles Dudley, and C.A. Hutchinson. *Post City, Texas: C.W. Post's Colonizing Activities in West Texas*. Foreword by Jesse H. Jones. Introduction by David J. Murrah. Post, TX: Garza County Historical Museum, 1998.

Ericson, Georgia Mae Smith, comp. *Aunt Hank's Rock House Kitchen: A Cook Book with a Story*. Crosbyton, TX: Crosby County Pioneer Memorial Museum and Crosby County Historical Commission, 1977.

Graves, Lawrence L., ed. *A History of Lubbock*. Lubbock: West Texas Museum Association, 1962.

Holden, W.C. *Rollie Burns: An Account of the Ranching Industry on the South Plains*. Dallas, TX: Southwest Press, 1932.

Kenner, Charles L. *The Comanchero Frontier: A History of New Mexican–Plains Indian Relations*. Norman: University of Oklahoma Press, 1994.

Morris, John Miller. *El Llano Estacado: Exploration and Imagination on the High Plains of Texas and New Mexico, 1536–1860*. Austin: Texas State Historical Association, 1997.

Murrah, David J. *"And Are We Yet Alive?" A History of the Northwest Texas Conference of the United Methodist Church*. Buffalo Gap, TX: State House Press, 2009.

———. *C.C. Slaughter: Rancher, Banker, Baptist*. Foreword by Cynthia Slaughter Pattison. Norman: University of Oklahoma Press, 2012.

———. *Oil, Taxes, and Cats: A History of the Devitt Family and the Mallet Ranch*. Lubbock: Texas Tech University Press, 1994.

Neugebauer, Janet M., ed. *Plains Farmer: The Diary of William G. DeLoach, 1914–1964*. College Station: Texas A&M University Press, 1991.

Rath, Ida Ellen. *The Rath Trail*. Wichita, KS: McCormick-Armstrong Co., Inc., 1961.

Tijerna, Andres A. *A History of Mexican Americans in Lubbock County, Texas*. Lubbock: Texas Tech University Press, 1979.

Wallace, Ernest. *Ranald S. Mackenzie on the Texas Frontier*. Foreword by David J. Murrah. College Station: Texas A&M University Press, 1993.

Index

C

D

I

J

K

L

M

S

T

U

V

W

X

Y

About the Contributors

Donald Abbe, PhD, is former curator of history at the Silent Wings Museum in Lubbock and historian of the Llano Estacado region.

J'Nell Pate Barnes, PhD, of Azle, Texas, is emeritus professor of history at Tarrant County College, author and Texas historian.

Jack Becker, MLS, MA, is a librarian at Texas Tech University and author of three books relating to West Texas.

Robert L. Carr, MD, of Lubbock is a retired physician, a prolific public speaker and a South Plains historian.

Henry Crawford, MA, recently retired as curator of history at the Museum of Texas Tech University.

Cheryl Lewis, RN, is a nurse, civic volunteer, bookstore owner and community historian in Hamlin, Texas.

Sylvia Gann Mahoney, MA, lives in Fort Worth and is an author, former college rodeo coach and promoter of the Great Western Cattle Trail.

Meredith McClain, PhD, retired from Texas Tech University in 2013 as emeritus associate professor of foreign languages.

JOHN MCCULLOUGH, MA, is an aviation historian, secretary of the Texas Aviation Heritage Foundation, Inc., and board member of the Silent Wings Museum.

DOLORES MOSSER of Lubbock is a children's book author and historian of the western Llano Estacado.

CURTIS PEOPLES, PHD, is archivist for Crossroads of Music Archives in the Southwest Collection/Special Collections Library at Texas Tech University.

ASHLEY PETTIET, MA, is curator of the King County Historical Museum and teaches social studies at Guthrie High School.

GENE B. PREUSS, PHD, is associate professor of history at the University of Houston–Downtown and a prolific author.

SAMMIE SIMPSON of Maple, Texas, is chief historian of Bailey County, Texas.

ROBERT SLEDGE, PHD, is emeritus distinguished professor of history at McMurry University in Abilene.

JENNIFER SPURRIER, EDD, is associate dean of libraries and director of the Southwest Collection at Texas Tech University.

JUNE STEELE, MA, teaches history and social studies at Monterey High School in Lubbock.

CHRISTENA STEPHENS, MS, is a writer, fine-art photographer, nonprofit geek and outdoor enthusiast living in Sundown, Texas.

LELAND TURNER, PHD, is a Fulbright Scholar and associate professor of history at Midwestern State University.

RANDY VANCE is manager of reference services at the Southwest Collection at Texas Tech University.

DONALD WALKER, PHD, was emeritus professor of history at Texas Tech University.

About the Editors

Paul H. Carlson, PhD, is a member of the Texas Institute of Letters and the Philosophical Society of Texas. As emeritus professor of history at Texas Tech University, he is the author of numerous books and articles and editor of others. A Fellow of both the Texas State Historical Association and the West Texas Historical Association, he is also the recipient of several university teaching awards. He lives with his wife, Ellen, in Ransom Canyon at the very edge of the Llano Estacado.

David J. Murrah, PhD, is a museum and historical consultant. He served for twenty-five years as archivist and director of the Southwest Collection at Texas Tech University before entering the museum exhibit/design field with Southwest Muscum Services of Houston. He has written or edited six books and numerous articles on Texas history and is a Fellow of both the Texas State Historical Association and the West Texas Historical Association. A native of the High Plains (Gruver, Texas), he and his wife, Ann, now live on the Texas coast at Rockport.

Visit us at
www.historypress.net